Ethics
in Psychotherapy
and Counseling

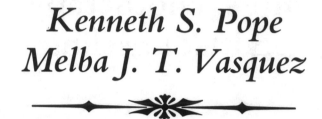

Kenneth S. Pope
Melba J. T. Vasquez

Ethics in Psychotherapy and Counseling

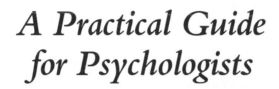

A Practical Guide for Psychologists

Jossey-Bass Publishers

San Francisco • Oxford • 1991

ETHICS IN PSYCHOTHERAPY AND COUNSELING
A Practical Guide for Psychologists
by Kenneth S. Pope and Melba J. T. Vasquez

Copyright © 1991 by: Jossey-Bass Inc., Publishers
                    350 Sansome Street
                    San Francisco, California 94104
                    &
                    Jossey-Bass Limited
                    Headington Hill Hall
                    Oxford OX3 0BW

Library of Congress Cataloging-in-Publication Data

Pope, Kenneth S.
   Ethics in psychotherapy and counseling : a practical guide for
psychologists / Kenneth S. Pope, Melba J. T. Vasquez.
      p.   cm. — (The Jossey-Bass social and behavioral science
series)
   Includes bibliographical references and index.
   ISBN 1-55542-347-7
   1. Counselors—Professional ethics.   2. Psychotherapists—
Professional ethics.   3. Counseling—Moral and ethical aspects.
4. Psychotherapy—Moral and ethical aspects.   5. Counselor and
client.   I. Vasquez, Melba Jean Trinidad.   II. Title.   III. Series.
BF637.C6P59   1991
174'.195—dc20   90-26036
                                                                 CIP

Manufactured in the United States of America

The paper in this book meets the guidelines for
permanence and durability of the Committee on
Production Guidelines for Book Longevity of
the Council on Library Resources.

Credits are on page 206.

JACKET DESIGN BY WILLI BAUM

FIRST EDITION

Code 9151

The Jossey-Bass
Social and Behavioral Science Series

For Alan, Alison, Gary, Janet, Laura, Paula,
Patti, Phil, and Pete,
whose courage, love, and kindness have meant
more than they will ever know
—Ken Pope

To Ofelia Vasquez Philo, the late Joe Vasquez, Jr.,
and Jim H. Miller—my models of integrity
—Melba Vasquez

Contents

Preface

Ethics are an essential guide for the work of psychotherapy and counseling. They are a process through which we awaken, enhance, inform, expand, and improve our ability to respond effectively to those who come to us for help.

Although they may be reflected in the formal standards of a professional association, in the civil or criminal law, or in the administrative guidelines of certification and licensing boards, ethics are not static codes. Such codes can call our attention to important values and mark off some of the extreme areas of unacceptable behavior, but they cannot do our thinking, feeling, and responding for us. Such codes can never be a substitute for the active process by which the individual therapist or counselor struggles with the sometimes bewildering, always unique constellation of responsibilities, contexts, and competing demands of helping another person.

We wrote this book to serve as a resource for that active, occasionally lonely, but potentially exciting process. *Ethics in Psychotherapy and Counseling* is based upon the premise that ethics are neither vague and lofty aspirations unrelated to the daily practicalities of the helping professions nor unvarying and coercive rules that preempt professionals' decisions and control their actions.

Solidly rooted in the research tradition, psychology is the only profession to use an empirical approach to creating its ethical standards. In 1948, the American Psychological Association (APA) surveyed all its members to ask what ethical challenges they faced in their day-to-day work. The responses identified over one thousand dilemmas that, carefully analyzed, became the basis of APA's first ethical standards.

APA's approach emphasized what is obvious to any therapist or counselor: Ethics must be practical. Clinicians confront an almost unimaginable diversity of situations, each with its own shifting demands and responsibilities. Every clinician is unique in important ways. Every client is unique in important ways. Ethics that are out of touch with the practical realities of clinical work, with the diversity and constantly changing nature of the therapeutic venture, are useless.

We wrote this book as a resource for those who are practicing, learning, or teaching psychotherapy. It grew out of our own work in those three roles.

In creating a resource that would be genuinely helpful to beginning and experienced clinicians, we believe that it is important to examine ethics not only as they are reflected in the formal professional codes but also as they are manifested in the actual work of the therapist. This book acknowledges and examines the complex interplay — and sometimes stark conflicts — among the needs of the client, the values of the therapist, the formal ethical standards, and the legal obligations. Attention is devoted to the external factors and complexities that can make recognizing and fulfilling ethical responsibilities seem so difficult and to those internal, very human tendencies that we all share, by which we deny, avoid, or distort the ethical implications of our behavior.

Audience

We wrote this book primarily for individuals who are doing, learning, or teaching therapy or counseling. While this text identifies ethical issues as they occur in actual practice and suggests possible approaches, it also provides a variety of open-ended vignettes and questions to prompt discussion in ethics courses, in clinical supervision and consultation, in staff meetings, or in workshops. We created the book as a resource not only for those in institutional settings (students and teachers in university courses, staff and trainees in clinics and hospitals) but also for those in independent practice. We hope that these "do-it-yourself" vignettes and questions will help independent practitioners by prompting or facilitating the formation of both formal and informal networks in which such questions are openly, candidly, and regularly discussed. Unfortunately, those of us in independent practice can easily become unnecessarily isolated from our colleagues and thus cut off from useful, frequent discussion of ethical challenges.

There is another reason for including these open-ended vignettes and questions: They emphasize the view that ethical awareness, deliberation, and behavior do not involve passive obedience or adherence to inflexible lists of "do's and don't's." The process is active and personal. Each therapist must struggle to create an ethical response to an individual client with individual needs within the context of a unique and constantly changing situation. All of us (except those who are omniscient, omnipotent, or sociopathic) feel overwhelmed at times because the work we have chosen to do and the responsibilities we have chosen to assume involve the irreducible complexity and frequently conflicting demands of human experience. Our work influences, sometimes in an extremely direct, profound, and immediate way, the lives of clients who may be hurting, unhappy, vulnerable, and perhaps in crisis. None of us is free from encountering unexpected, unfamiliar clinical situations for which there are no clear answers. What is crucial is that we continue our active involvement in the process of informed ethical awareness, analysis, and struggle.

Overview of the Contents

Chapter One addresses the fundamental ethical challenge we all face in our day-to-day work with clients: how to be helpful without hurting. The chapter identifies typical ways in which we creatively rationalize unethical behavior by denying our responsibilities and explores how we can become more aware of the ethical responsibilities inherent in our work.

Both the professions themselves (through ethics committees) and society more generally (through licensing boards and the civil and criminal courts) have attempted to create formal mechanisms to ensure that clinicians fulfill their responsibility to help without hurting. Chapter Two provides historical, descriptive, and actuarial information regarding these mechanisms. For example, actuarial data, classified according to cause of complaint, are presented for ethics complaints, licensing actions, and malpractice suits involving psychologists. Clinicians often feel caught between the conflicting demands of ethical and legal codes; we discuss the implications of survey research for this dilemma.

Chapter Three explores the three inherent aspects of the relationship between therapist or counselor and client: trust, power, and caring.

Chapter Four identifies six beliefs about psychotherapy or ethics which, *in their most extreme forms,* can make us more vulnerable to overlooking the ethical implications of our work. These six beliefs are psychotherapy as scientific technology, psychotherapy as mystery, psychotherapy as business, ethics as adherence to legal and administrative standards, ethics as rare dramatic conflict, and ethics as mindless rule following.

Chapter Five discusses the ethical responsibility to practice within areas of demonstrable competence. We review factors that interfere with fulfilling this responsibility, as well as those that help the clinician practice competently.

Chapter Six examines such questions as When does an individual become a client? What constitutes formal termination of therapy? What access does a client have a right to expect from a therapist? and How can therapist and client plan for a crisis in which the therapist is unavailable?

Chapter Seven discusses the complex legal and ethical aspects of the client's right to informed consent to treatment and to informed refusal of treatment. An impressive body of empirical research can provide guidance to clinicians in this area.

Chapter Eight focuses on ethical issues related to testing,

diagnosis, and assessment. Among the topics covered are staying within areas of competence; understanding measurement, validation, and research; respecting the client's rights to informed consent or informed refusal; clarifying access to test reports and raw data; following standard procedures for administering tests; being aware of personal and financial factors leading to misusing diagnosis; understanding gender effects and cultural influences; acknowledging the low base rate phenomenon; paying attention to potential medical causes; knowing about prior records of assessment and treatment; explicitly indicating all reservations concerning reliability and validity; and staying current.

Chapter Nine discusses sexual relationships with clients. It reviews the issues and relevant research concerning injured clients, perpetrators, nonsexual physical contact with clients, sexual attraction to clients, responding to victimized clients, and rehabilitation.

Chapter Ten explores nonsexual dual relationship issues, reviewing ethical and legal aspects as well as the empirical research studies. The chapter examines common strategies by which therapists tend to justify engaging in unethical dual relationships with their clients, such as selective inattention, hypothetical benefits, prevalence, tradition, client autonomy, and necessity.

Chapter Eleven focuses on ethical issues related to culture, context, and individual differences. Topics include acknowledging socioeconomic differences, remaining alert to possible bias in interpreting research, potential problems with assessment instruments and with interaction process, understanding the context, and creativity.

Chapter Twelve discusses ethical responsibilities and dilemmas related to confidentiality. Topics include waivers of confidentiality; legal requirements to divulge confidential information; informing the patient about limitations to confidentiality; insurance forms; communications involving psychological assistants and interns; case notes and client files; disposing of charts; phone messages; referral sources; gossip; published case studies; and confidentiality of test materials.

Chapter Thirteen addresses issues relevant to assessing suicidal risk and intervening with suicidal clients. It reviews research and risk factors, covers special considerations in working with suicidal clients, and identifies avoidable pitfalls.

Chapter Fourteen explores ethical aspects of supervision. Topics include clear tasks, roles, and responsibilities; competence; assessment and evaluation of supervisees; informed consent; sexual issues; and establishing guidelines and coverage plans.

A Note on Terminology

This book addresses ethical issues encountered by psychologists functioning as *therapists* and *counselors*. For the sake of brevity and convenience, we have often used one term or the other rather than both in a given sentence. Similarly, some psychologists identify those to whom they provide services as *clients;* others use the term *patients*. Again, for the sake of brevity and convenience, we have used these terms interchangeably throughout the book.

Acknowledgments

We are indebted to the many individuals who contributed, directly or indirectly, to this book. We are grateful to all, but space limitations allow us to mention only a few by name. Ursula Delworth, Gerald Koocher, and Janet Sonne carefully reviewed an earlier draft of the manuscript and offered valuable suggestions for improving it. Sandra Haber and Karen Zager, former and current editors, respectively, of the American Psychological Association Division 42's *Independent Practitioner,* helped improve certain portions of this book that appeared previously in that journal. Finally, we greatly appreciate the exceptionally capable and generous help we have received from Rebecca McGovern and Xenia Lisanevich of Jossey-Bass Publishers.

March 1991   Kenneth S. Pope
                                                Los Angeles, California

                                                Melba J. T. Vasquez
                                                Austin, Texas

The Authors

Kenneth S. Pope is in independent practice as a psychotherapist in Los Angeles. He received his M.A. degree (1972) from Harvard University in English literature and his Ph.D. degree (1977) from Yale University in clinical psychology. He is a diplomate in clinical psychology and a fellow of the American Psychological Association and the American Psychological Society.

He has coedited two books, *The Stream of Consciousness: Scientific Investigations into the Flow of Human Experience* (1978, with J. L. Singer) and *The Power of Human Imagination: New Methods of Psychotherapy* (1978, with J. L. Singer). He is the author of *On Love and Loving: Psychological Perspectives on the Nature and Experience of Romantic Love* (1980, with others) and *Sexual Intimacies Between Therapists and Patients* (1986, with J. C. Bouhoutsos). A journal editor, he has published numerous research articles, many in the area of ethics and malpractice. He is a recipient of the Belle Mayer Bromberg Award for Literature and the Frances Mosseker Award for Fiction.

He previously served as chair of the Ethics Committees of the American Psychological Association and the American Board of Professional Psychology. He taught courses in abnormal psychology, psychological and neuropsychological assessment, and professional standards of care at the University of

California, Los Angeles, where he served as a psychotherapy supervisor in the UCLA Psychology Clinic. His prior experience also includes serving as clinical director and psychology director in both private hospital and community mental health center settings.

Melba J. T. Vasquez is senior psychologist at the Counseling and Mental Health Center, University of Texas, Austin, and is in independent practice as a therapist. She received her Ph.D. degree (1978) from the University of Texas, Austin, in counseling psychology. She is a diplomate in counseling psychology and a fellow of the American Psychological Association. She is a recipient of the 1989 Teaching and Training Award from the American Psychological Association's Minority Fellowship Program. Her research and publication have focused primarily on women's concerns, ethnic minority psychology, training and supervision, and professional ethics.

Vasquez has served as director of internship training at Colorado State University and the University of Texas, Austin, and has been a member of several editorial boards. She has taught graduate courses in multicultural issues in psychology, professional ethics, and counseling and psychotherapy. She served on the Ethics Committee of the American Psychological Association (APA), the APA Task Force for Revision of Ethical Principles, the APA Board of Social and Ethical Responsibility, the APA Task Force on Sexual Impropriety in Psychology, the APA Committee on Women in Psychology, and the APA Board for the Advancement of Psychology in the Public Interest. She also chaired a task force for the Board of Ethnic Minority Affairs.

Ethics
in Psychotherapy
and Counseling

1

Helping Without Hurting: Enhancing Ethical Awareness

Psychotherapy and counseling hold out the promise of help for people who are hurting and in need. When the process works as it is supposed to, lives can be changed in lasting and profound ways. Clients can gain awareness and understanding of themselves and their lives. They can confront traumas and tragedies and come to terms with these events in a way that will not leave them numb or paralyzed. They can become happier and more fulfilled or at least less miserable. They can learn new behaviors as well as how to teach themselves new behaviors. They can learn to trust or to trust more wisely. They can become more aware of what values they affirm, what makes their life meaningful. They can develop a sense of well-being and become better able, as Freud noted, to love and to work.

Ethics and Responsibility

Our ethics acknowledge the great responsibilities inherent in the promise and process of our profession. They reflect the fact that if we do not fulfill these responsibilities with the greatest care, people may be hurt.

Our work as therapists and counselors may make a crucial difference in whether a young child's history of incest is ac-

1

curately recognized and addressed, whether a battered spouse is able to find a safe environment or remains in a potentially lethal setting, and whether a client loses hope and commits suicide or continues to live, to name but a few examples. Even therapists at the beginning of their careers are aware that such focused and dramatic examples tell only part of the story. So many people who come to us for help face much more elusive, mundane, and sometimes seemingly trivial problems, yet the arduous, risky, and frequently discouraging course of their therapy may play a key role in their struggle to lead more meaningful, more effective, more personally fulfilling lives.

Few therapists take this responsibility lightly. Few are able to set aside their concern about a suicidal client between sessions. Few sit unmoved while a client is recounting, often with great emotion, a traumatic event that has just come into awareness after a long period of forgetfulness.

This very human ability to be moved by the dilemmas and struggles of another human being and the sense of responsibility we feel regarding our attempts to help at times feel like a tremendous weight upon our shoulders. Our work can evoke anxiety and a sense of great uncertainty. Unfortunately, it can also make us more vulnerable to additional sources of stress inherent in our attempts to help.

One additional source of stress for some of us is the fact that there is no by-the-book, one-size-fits-all guide to responding to a client's clinical needs. Whether increasing the number of weekly sessions from two to four during a crisis would help or hurt (or, less likely, have no net effect) is a decision that must be made on the basis of professional judgment regarding the individual situation of the client. Whether providing a stressed client with imagery techniques designed to reduce stress would ultimately be more helpful for a given client (helping the client to become less distressed and therefore more functional) or possibly harmful (facilitating the client's adjustment to an abusive work or home environment) is a question to which there is no instantly clear and universally accepted answer. The inescapable responsibility of rendering careful, informed professional judgments regarding issues of enormous complexity can, especially when we are feeling stress from other sources, be a burden.

Another additional source of stress for some of us is the fear that we will be held accountable, after the fact, by formal review agencies. Some agencies, such as local, state, and national professional ethics committees, focus specifically on the ethical aspects of our work. Others, such as state licensing boards and the civil courts, seek to enforce professional standards of care that may embody ethical principles and responsibilities. Many of us tend to react to the possibility of facing a formal complaint with something approaching panic.

Still another source of stress can be the process of learning or supervising therapy and counseling. As supervisors, we may be uncomfortable with how the supervisee responds to the client differently from how we would, with our obligation to evaluate the supervisee's work, and with the demands of our role as teacher and mentor. As supervisees, we may be doubtful of our ability to assume clinical responsibilities (especially when they involve suicidal or homicidal risks), fearful of making mistakes, frustrated by differences in values or theoretical orientation between ourselves and our supervisor, and concerned that if we are completely truthful in describing to our supervisor what we actually thought, felt, and did with our clients, we might be advised to look for another line of work.

The following six fictional scenarios were created for a series of ethics and malpractice workshops. None of the hypothetical vignettes is based on an actual or specific case (and none of the individuals is based upon an actual clinician or patient), but all the scenarios represent the kinds of challenges faced by therapists and counselors. In these scenarios, each clinician was attempting to do his or her best. Readers may disagree over whether the clinician met the highest or even minimal ethical standards, and such disagreements can form the focus of classroom, case conference, supervision, or related discussions. In at least one or two instances, you may conclude that what the clinician did was perfectly reasonable and perhaps even showed courage and sensitivity. In some cases, you may feel that significant relevant information is missing. But in each instance, the professional's actions (or failures to act) become the basis of one or more formal complaints.

Fictional Scenario 1

Mr. Alvarez, a thirty-five-year-old professor of physics, has never before sought psychotherapy. He shows up for his first appointment with Dr. Brinks. Mr. Alvarez says that his life is in chaos. He was granted full professor status about a year ago and about one month after that, his wife suddenly left him to live with another man. He became very depressed. About four months ago, he began to become anxious and to have trouble concentrating. He feels he needs someone to talk to so that he can figure out what happened. Mr. Alvarez and Dr. Brinks agree to meet twice every week for outpatient psychotherapy.

During the first few sessions, Mr. Alvarez says that he feels relieved that he can talk about his problems, but he remains very anxious. During the next few months, he begins talking about some traumatic experiences in his early childhood. He reports that he is having even more trouble concentrating. Dr. Brinks assures him that this is not surprising, that problems concentrating often become temporarily worse when a patient starts becoming aware of painful memories that had been repressed. She suggests that they begin meeting three times a week, and Mr. Alvarez agrees.

One month later, Mr. Alvarez collapses, is rushed to the hospital, but is dead upon arrival. An autopsy reveals that a small but growing tumor had been pressing against a blood vessel in his brain. When the vessel burst, he died.

Months after Mr. Alvarez's death, Dr. Brinks is served notice that the state ethics committee is opening a formal case against her based upon a complaint filed by Mr. Alvarez's relatives. Furthermore, she is being sued for malpractice. The ethics complaint and the malpractice suit allege that she was negligent in diagnosing Mr. Alvarez in that she had failed to take any step to rule out organic causes for Mr. Alvarez's concentration difficulties, had not applied any of the principles and procedures of the profession of psychology to identify organic impairment, and had not referred Mr. Alvarez for evaluation by a neuropsychologist or to a physician for a medical examination.

Psychotherapists and counselors in ethics and malpractice workshops (who would probably *not* constitute a random sample of practicing psychologists) who have reviewed scenario 1 have tended to conclude that Dr. Brinks may have been functioning beyond the range of her competence (see Chapter Five) and violated some of the fundamental standards of assessment (see Chapter Eight).

Fictional Scenario 2

Ms. Cain brings her two children, ages four and six, to Dr. Durrenberger for a psychological evaluation. She reports that they have become somewhat upset during the last few months. They are having nightmares and frequently wet their beds. She suspects that the problem may have something to do with their last visit with their father, who lives in another state.

Dr. Durrenberger schedules three sessions in which he sees Ms. Cain and her two children together and three individual sessions with each of the children. As he is preparing his report, he receives a subpoena to testify in a civil suit that Ms. Cain is filing against her ex-husband. She is suing for custody of her children. During the trial, Dr. Durrenberger testifies that the children seem, on the basis of interviews and psychological tests, to have a stronger, more positive relationship with their mother. He gives his professional opinion that the children would be better off with their mother and that she should be given custody.

Mr. Cain files an ethics complaint, a civil suit, and a licensing complaint against Dr. Durrenberger. One basis of his complaint is that Dr. Durrenberger had not obtained informed consent to conduct the assessments. When Mr. and Ms. Cain had divorced two years previously, the court had granted Mr. Cain legal custody of the children but had granted Ms. Cain visitation rights. (Ms. Cain had arranged for the assessments of the children during a long summer visit.) Another basis of the complaint was that Dr. Durrenberger had made a formal recommendation regarding custody placement without making any attempt to interview or evaluate Mr. Cain. Mr. Cain's attorney and expert witnesses maintained that no custody recommendation could be made without interviewing both parents.

Although laws regarding rights of custodial and noncustodial parents differ from state to state, participants in ethics and malpractice workshops tend to conclude that Dr. Durrenberger had not fulfilled his ethical (and in many states, legal) responsibility to obtain adequate informed consent from the relevant parent (see Chapter Seven) and that he had failed to conduct an adequate assessment to justify his conclusion (see Chapter Eight).

Fictional Scenario 3

When George, a nineteen-year-old college student, began psychotherapy with Dr. Hightower, he told the doctor that he was suffering from a fatal disease. Two months into therapy, George felt that he trusted his therapist enough to tell her that the disease was AIDS.

During the next eighteen months, much of the therapy focused on George's losing battle with his illness and his preparations to die. After two stays in the hospital for pneumonia, George informed Dr. Hightower that he knew he would not survive his next hospitalization. He had done independent research and talked with his physicians, and he was certain that, if pneumonia developed again, it would be fatal due to numerous complications and that it would likely be a long and painful death. George said that when that time came, he wanted to die in the off-campus apartment he had lived in since he came to college — not in the hospital. He would, when he felt himself getting sicker, take some illicitly obtained drugs that would ease him into death. Dr. Hightower tried to dissuade him from this plan, but George refused to discuss it and said that if Dr. Hightower continued to bring up the subject, he would quit therapy. Convinced that George would quit therapy rather than discuss his plan, Dr. Hightower decided that the best course of action was to offer caring and support — rather than confrontation and argument — to a patient who seemed to have only a few months to live.

Four months later, Dr. Hightower was notified that George had taken his life. Within the next month, Dr. Hightower became the defendant in two civil suits. One suit, filed by George's family, alleged that Dr. Hightower, aware that George was intending to take his own life, did not take reasonable and adequate steps to prevent the suicide, that she had not notified any third parties of the suicide plan, had not required George to get rid of the illicit drugs, and had not used hospitalization to prevent the suicide. The other suit was filed by a college student who had been George's lover. The student alleged that Dr. Hightower, knowing that George had a lover and that he had a fatal sexually transmitted disease, had a duty to protect the lover. The lover alleged ignorance that George had been suffering from AIDS.

This scenario has been one of the most agonizing and controversial for the psychotherapists and counselors who consider it at ethics and malpractice workshops. Some believe that Dr. Hightower acted in the most humane, sensitive, and ethical manner; others believe that she was wrong to accept, without more vigorous challenge, George's decision to take his own life. In this sense, it illustrates the dilemmas we face when confronted with a suicidal individual (see Chapter Thirteen). It also illustrates how such issues as confidentiality (see Chapter Twelve) have been challenged when a specific third party or the public more generally is perceived to be put at risk by a client.

Fictional Scenario 4

Ms. Huang, whose family had moved from mainland China to the United States fifteen years ago, is a forty-five-year-old automobile mechanic. She agreed, at the strong urging of her employer, to seek psychotherapy for difficulties that seem to affect her work. She has been showing up late at her job, has often phoned in sick, and frequently appears distracted. She complains to her new therapist, Dr. Jackson, of the difficulties of coping both with psychomotor epilepsy, which has been controlled through medication, and with her progressive diabetes, for which she is also receiving medical care.

Although she has no real experience treating those from the Chinese culture or those with chronic medical conditions such as epilepsy, Dr. Jackson begins to work with Ms. Huang. She meets with her on a regular basis for three months, but never feels that a solid working alliance is developing. After three months, Ms. Huang abruptly quits therapy. At the time, she has not paid for the last six sessions.

Two weeks later, Dr. Jackson receives a request to send Ms. Huang's treatment records to her new therapist. Dr. Jackson notifies Ms. Huang that she will not forward the records until the bill has been paid in full.

Some time later, Dr. Jackson is notified that she is the complainee in an ethics case opened by the Ethics Committee of the American Psychological Association (APA) and that she has been sued for malpractice. The complaints allege that Dr. Jackson had been practicing outside of her areas of competence because she had received no formal education or training and had no supervised experience in treating people from the Chinese culture or those with multiple serious and chronic medical diseases. The complaints also alleged that Ms. Huang had never adequately understood the nature of treatment as evidenced by the lack of any written informed consent. Finally, the complaints alleged that "holding records hostage" for payment violated Ms. Huang's welfare and deprived her subsequent therapist of having prompt and comprehensive information necessary to Ms. Huang's treatment.

Participants in ethics and malpractice workshops, asked to assume the role of an ethics committee to review this scenario, tend to conclude that Dr. Jackson was acting without adequate competence (see Chapter Five) to treat someone from a different culture (see Chapter Eleven) or with a chronic medical condition, had not obtained adequate consent (see Chapter Seven), and had misused the power of her role as therapist (see Chapter Three).

Fictional Scenario 5

Dr. Larson is executive director and clinical chief of staff at the Golden Internship Psychotherapy Center. For one year, he closely supervises an excellent postdoctoral intern, Dr. Marshall. The supervisee shows great potential, working with a range of patients who respond positively to her interventions. After completing her internship and becoming licensed, Dr. Marshall goes into business for herself, opening an office several blocks from Golden Internship Psychotherapy Center. Before terminating her work at the center, Dr. Larson tells Dr. Marshall that she must transfer all patients to other center therapists. All of the patients who can afford her fee schedule, however, decide to continue in therapy with Dr. Marshall at her new office. The patients who cannot afford Dr. Marshall's fee schedule are assigned to new therapists at the center. Dr. Larson hires an attorney to take legal action against Dr. Marshall, asserting that she unethically exploited the center by stealing patients and engaging in deceptive practices. He files formal complaints against her with both the state licensing board and the APA Ethics Committee, charging that she had refused to follow his supervision in regard to the patients and pointed out that he, as the clinical supervisor of this trainee, had been both clinically and legally responsible for the patients. He refuses to turn over the patients' charts to Dr. Marshall or to certify to various associations to whom she has applied for membership that Dr. Marshall has successfully completed her internship.

Dr. Marshall countersues, claiming that Dr. Larson is engaging in illegal restraint of trade and not acting in the patients' best interests. The patients, she asserts, have formed an intense transference and an effective working alliance with her; to lose their therapist would be clinically damaging and not in their best interests. She files formal complaints against Dr. Larson with the licensing board and the APA Ethics Committee, charging that his refusal to deliver copies of the patients' charts and to certify that she completed the internship violates ethical and professional standards.

Some of the patients sue the center, Dr. Larson, and Dr. Marshall, charging that the conflict and the legal actions (in which their cases are put at issue without their consent) have been damaging to their therapy.

Workshop participants have tended to conclude that both Dr. Larson and Dr. Marshall have behaved unethically in terms of misusing their power (see Chapter Three), failing to clarify in advance the conclusion of Dr. Marshall's work with the patients (see Chapter Six), and neglecting to address these issues adequately in the supervisory contract (see Chapter Fourteen).

Fictional Scenario 6

In therapy for one year with Dr. Franks, Mr. Edwards is alcoholic and drank heavily for four years prior to the therapy. Dr. Franks uses a psychodynamic approach but also incorporates behavioral techniques specifically designed to address the drinking problem.

Two months into therapy, when it became apparent that outpatient psychotherapy alone was not effective, Mr. Edwards agreed to attend Alcoholics Anonymous (AA) meetings as an adjunct to his therapy. During the past nine months of therapy, Mr. Edwards had generally been sober, suffering only two relapses, each time falling off the wagon for a long weekend.

Now, a year into therapy, Mr. Edwards suffers a third relapse. He comes to the session having just had several drinks. During the session, Dr. Franks and Mr. Edwards conclude that some of the troubling material that has been emerging in the therapy had led Mr. Edwards to begin drinking again. At the end of the session, Mr. Edwards feels that he has gained some additional insight into why he drank. He decides to go straight from the session to an AA meeting.

One month later, Dr. Franks is notified that he is being sued. On his way from the therapy session to the AA meeting, Mr. Edwards had run a red light and had killed a mother and her child who were crossing the street. The suit alleged that the therapist knew or should have known his patient to be dangerous and should have taken steps to prevent him from driving until his alcoholism no longer constituted a danger to the public.

Although workshop participants tend to fault Dr. Franks for not adequately assessing his client's condition and the danger that the client's driving in that condition would constitute for the public (see Chapter Eight), there was a common empathetic response, as with many of the other scenarios. Clinicians tended to identify with the fictional Dr. Franks and thought, "There, but for the grace of God, go I." Struck by the enormous complexity and responsibilities the clinicians face in these secnarios, we wonder if we would do any better were we in their places and if we are doing any better in our own practices (our failures of responsibility perhaps being in different areas though just as serious).

Each scenario tends to bring home the reality that formal mechanisms of accountability act to protect clients from unethical and potentially harmful practices (see Chapter Two), but may also increase the stress that we feel at the possibility that one day we may be the subject of a formal complaint.

Yet another source of stress for some of us is the sense that, in some areas at least, the responsibilities to which we are held accountable do not seem matched by our abilities and resources. For example, society (through the courts) may hold us accountable for predicting and preventing homicide. But accurately predicting whether someone will or will not kill seems to be beyond the capacity of mental health professionals or anyone else, for that matter (see Chapter Eight).

In the midst of all this responsibility, complexity, uncertainty, and stress, remaining alert to the ethical aspects of our work in a consistent and meaningful manner can seem overwhelming.

Ethics and Denial

If staying alert to ethical aspects and fulfilling the ethical responsibilities of our work overwhelm us, or if we are personally overwhelmed by other factors so that we are unable to be ethically responsible, all of us are vulnerable to denial and other ways of dismissing, distorting, or discounting ethical questions as they threaten to become prominent or even noticeable. We all have our favored ways of making uncomfortable ethical challenges disappear, perhaps by transforming them almost magically into something else, perhaps by attacking the client or colleague who raises the ethical question, perhaps by viewing ourselves as helpless, as compelled by necessity to act in a way that we suspect may be unethical. Take a few minutes to conduct a private self-assessment of the degree to which these forms of ethical denial may have infiltrated your own practice as a therapist, counselor, supervisor, or trainee.

For the therapist, counselor, supervisor, or trainee, professional ethics represent three basic tasks (discussed more fully in Chapter Three). First, professional ethics involve acknowledging the reality and importance of the individuals whose lives we affect by our professional actions. Second, they involve understanding the nature of the professional relationship and professional interventions. Third, they involve affirming accountability for our behavior.

A moment of active and honest self-assessment can give us at least a general sense of the degree to which we are accomplishing these tasks effectively, regardless of whether we are graduate students, interns, new licensees, seasoned veterans, or supervisors.

Are the people whom we serve real to us? To what extent do we misuse valid diagnostic and classification systems in a way that diminishes clients? Do we think of three clients not so much as individuals but as the two schizophrenics and the one borderline? To what extent do we view them as somehow inferior humans because they are clients? If we are in independent practice, have we begun thinking of our clients less as individuals to be helped than as sources of payment for office overhead?

To what extent do we maintain an adequate awareness of the nature and implications of the professional relationship and of our professional interventions? Have we become insensitive to the trust with which so many of our clients invest their relationship to us, of the degree to which they count on us for hope and help? Have we begun to blur the professional boundaries so that certain clients are no longer sure whether they are our clients or our business partners, friends, or lovers?

To what extent do we hold ourselves accountable not only for what we do but also for what we fail to do as professionals? Do we tend to shift all responsibility onto the bureaucracy of the organization for which we work? Do we assume because we have not been subject to any formal complaint procedures that therefore we have been behaving in an ethically exemplary manner? Do we attempt to use the complexity of our work as a cloak to conceal the responsibilities that we have failed to fulfill?

This general self-assessment may be supplemented with a more specific assessment of the degree to which we use common fallacies and rationalizations to justify our unethical behavior and to quiet a noisy conscience. These attempts to disguise unethical behavior might be termed *ethical substandards,* although they are in no way ethical and many are so far beneath the standards of the profession that "sub-" seems an understatement. They can make even the most hurtful and reprehensible behaviors seem ethical, or at least insignificant. All of us, at one time or another, probably have endorsed at least some of them. And all of us could probably extend the list. If some excuses seem absurd and humorous to us, it is likely that we have not yet had to resort to using those particular rationalizations. At some future moment of great stress or exceptional temptation, those funny absurdities may gain considerable plausibility if not a comforting certitude. Such substandards we commonly use to justify the unjustifiable include the following:

1. It's not unethical as long as you don't talk about ethics. The principle of general denial is at work here. As long as neither you nor your colleagues mention ethical aspects of practice, no course of action could be identified as unethical.

2. It's not unethical as long as you don't know a law, ethical principle, or professional standard that prohibits it. This substandard encompasses two principles: specific ignorance and specific literalization. The principle of specific ignorance states that even if there is, say, a law prohibiting an action, what you do is not illegal as long as you are unaware of the law. The principle of literalization states that if you cannot find specific mention of a particular incident anywhere in legal, ethical, or professional standards, it must be ethical.

3. It's not unethical as long as you can name at least five other clinicians—right off the top of your head—who do the same thing. (There are probably countless thousands more whom you don't know about or whom you could name if you just had the time.)

4. It's not unethical as long as none of your clients has ever complained about it.

5. It's not unethical as long as your client wanted you to do it.

6. It's not unethical as long as your clients' condition (probably borderline) made them so difficult to treat and so

troublesome and risky to be around that they elicited whatever it was you did (not, of course, to admit that you actually did anything).

7. It's not unethical as long as you weren't really feeling well that day and thus couldn't be expected to perform up to your usual level of quality.

8. It's not unethical as long as a friend of yours knew someone who said that an ethics committee somewhere once issued an opinion that it's o.k.

9. It's not unethical as long as you're sure that legal, ethical, and professional standards were made up by people who don't understand the hard realities of psychological practice.

10. It's not unethical as long as it results in a higher income or more prestige.

11. It's not unethical as long as it's more convenient than doing things another way.

12. It's not unethical as long as no one else finds out — or if whoever might find out probably wouldn't care anyway.

13. It's not unethical as long as you're observing most of the other ethical standards. This means that everyone can, by fiat, nullify one or two ethical principles as long as the other *more important* standards are observed. In a pinch, it's o.k. to observe a majority of the standards. In a real emergency, it's acceptable simply to have observed one of the ethical principles in some situation at some time in your life. Or to have thought about observing it.

14. It's not unethical as long as there's no intent to do harm.

15. It's not unethical as long as there is no body of universally accepted, scientific studies showing, without any doubt whatsoever, that *exactly* what you did was the sole cause of harm to the client. This view was vividly and succinctly stated by a member of the Texas pesticide regulatory board charged with protecting Texas citizens against undue risks from pesticides. In discussing Chlordane, a chemical used to kill termites, one member said, "Sure, it's going to kill a lot of people, but they may be dying of something else anyway" ("Perspectives," 1990, p. 17).

16. It's not unethical as long as you don't intend to do it more than once.
17. It's not unethical as long as no one can prove you did it.
18. It's not unethical as long as you're an important person. The criteria for importance generally include being rich, well-known, extensively published, or tenured, having a large practice, possessing substantial malpractice liability coverage, or knowing personally someone who, in retrospect, thought APA's purchase of *Psychology Today* was a good idea.
19. It's not unethical as long as you're busy. After all, given your work load and responsibilities, who could reasonably expect you to obtain informed consent from all your clients, keep your chart notes in a secured area, be thorough when conducting assessments, or follow every little law?

Even if these self-serving defenses, rationalizations, and phony justifications fail to protect us from at least some sense that we are engaging in unethical behavior, memory may take care of the discomfort. At the end of Woody Allen's film *Crimes and Misdemeanors,* the doctor played by Martin Landau talks about a monumental event in his life: His mistress had threatened to make public their affair; he had arranged to have her murdered. He speaks with obvious fascination of how he had expected the event to haunt him for the rest of his life. However, he had found that each day the memory had bothered him a little less; the memory faded and ceased to carry any impact. He was, in fact, far happier than he had ever been.

Cognitive psychology has demonstrated the amazing degree to which our memories become altered to fit the schemas (or images) we have of ourselves. Interested readers may want to read Neisser's (1981) fascinating account of the workings of John Dean's memory. During the Watergate hearings, Dean appeared to have a remarkably accurate and detailed memory — virtually photographic. Neisser compared Dean's testimony about conversations with President Nixon to the actual tapes of those conversations, which were only released later. The memory errors were systematic: Dean's memory had distorted events to make himself appear better, more important. Our selective and malleable memory is always available to ensure that ethical unease about a particular incident can fade.

Ethical Awakening

We use the ethical substandards and other mechanisms of denial to dull and quiet our concerns, to lull our conscience, ethical judgment, and sensitivity to sleep. At least occasionally, ethical responsibilities can make such demands on our integrity and can become so pressing, troubling, and painful that we seek any avenue of escape. We want to get rid of the responsibility or at least of the awareness of the responsibility.

But the necessity of awakening ourselves to the ethical aspects of each new clinical situation remains constant. There is no realistic or legitimate way to spare ourselves the continuing process of examining, identifying, and attempting to address the ethical challenges of our work. Our shared and very human vulnerability to denial and the other defenses we use to protect ourselves from this process (at the expense of our clients, our work, and ourselves) is a major focus of this book. In addressing various topics, the book will highlight some of the maneuvers by which we commonly try to avoid acknowledging and fulfilling our ethical responsibilities.

The ethical codes and formal ethical principles are a crucial resource in this process of ethical awakening. But they are not a substitute for an active, deliberative, and creative approach to fulfilling our ethical responsibilities. They prompt, guide, and inform rather than preclude our ethical considerations.

There is no way that the codes and principles can be effectively followed or applied in a rote, thoughtless manner. Each new client, whatever his or her similarities to previous clients, is a unique individual. Each situation also is unique and is likely to change significantly over time.

The explicit codes and principles may designate numerous possible approaches as clearly unethical. They may identify with greater or lesser degrees of clarity the types of ethical concerns that are likely to be especially significant, but they cannot tell us how these concerns will manifest themselves in a particular clinical situation. They may set forth essential tasks that we must fulfill, but they cannot tell us how we can accomplish these tasks with a unique client facing unique problems. Because the formal ethical codes and related means of accountability play a significant role in prompting, guiding, and informing our ethical deliberations, we turn our attention to them in Chapter Two.

2

Ethical and Legal Codes and Complaints: Historical and Actuarial Foundations

As psychotherapists and counselors, we are members of the mental health profession. Exactly what we have to profess has been the subject for debate from the beginning. We have always had difficulty defining what we do.

The Boulder Conference conducted one of the most intense efforts to define psychotherapy so it could be effectively taught to clinical and counseling psychologists. Carl Rogers, president of the American Psychological Association in 1947, had appointed David Shakow to chair a committee on defining and teaching psychotherapy. The Shakow report, adopted at the 1947 APA convention, resulted in the Boulder Conference two years later. On August 28, 1949, the recorder for the Boulder task force for defining psychotherapy and setting forth criteria for adequate training provided the following summary: "We have left therapy as an undefined technique which is applied to unspecified problems with a nonpredictable outcome. For this technique we recommend rigorous training" (Lehner, 1952, p. 547).

Mechanisms of Accountability

Difficulties in defining domains and activities, however, do not release any profession from the primary responsibility of setting forth its ethics. The hallmark of a profession is the recognition that the work its members carry out influences, sometimes in an extremely direct, profound, and immediate way, the lives of their clients. The powerful nature of this influence makes the customary rules of the marketplace (often resting on variations of the principle "Let the buyer beware") inadequate (see Chapter Three). Society asks that the profession set forth a code to which the members of the profession agree to be held accountable. At its heart, this code calls for the professional to protect and promote the welfare of clients and to avoid letting the professional's self-interests place the client at risk for harm.

Perhaps because society would never put *complete* trust in professions to enforce their own standards and perhaps because the professions have demonstrated that they, at least occasionally, are less than vigorous, scrupulous, and effective in governing their own behavior, society has established additional means for attempting to ensure that professions meet minimal standards as they carry out their work and that those who are served by professionals are protected from the iatrogenic harm that can result from incompetent, negligent, and unscrupulous practitioners.

Four major mechanisms hold psychotherapists and counselors formally accountable to an explicit set of professional standards: professional ethics committees, state licensing boards, civil (for example, malpractice) courts, and criminal courts. Each of these four mechanisms uses a different formulation of standards, though there may be substantial overlap. Behavior may be clearly unethical and yet not form the basis for criminal charges.

In some cases, psychotherapists and counselors may feel an agonizing conflict among these sets of standards. They may, for example, feel that the law compels them to act in a way that violates the welfare of the client and the clinician's own sense of what is ethical. A national survey of psychologists found that a majority (57 percent) of the respondents had intentionally violated the law or a similar formal standard because, in their opinion, not to do so would have injured the client or violated some deeper value (Pope & Bajt, 1988). The actions reported by two or more respondents included refusing to report child abuse (21 percent), illegally divulging confidential information (21 percent), engaging in sex with a patient (9 percent), engaging in nonsexual dual relationships (6 percent), and refusing to make legally required warnings regarding dangerous patients (6 percent).

That almost one out of ten of the participants reported engaging in sex with a client (see Chapter Nine) using the rationale of patient welfare or deeper moral value highlights the risks, ambiguities, and difficulties of evaluating the degree to which our own individual behavior is ethical. Pope and Bajt (1988) reviewed the attempts of philosophers and the courts to address the issue of the individual deciding to go against the law. On the one hand, for example, the U.S. Supreme Court emphasized that in the United States no one could be considered higher than the law: "In the fair administration of justice no man can be judge in his own case, however exalted his station, however righteous his motives, and irrespective of his race, color, politics, or religion" (*Walker v. City of Birmingham,* 1967, pp. 1219–1220).

On the other hand, however, courts endorsed Thoreau's (1849/1960) injunction that if a law "requires you to be the agent of injustice to another, then . . . break the law" (p. 242). The California Supreme Court, for example, tacitly condoned violation of the law *only when the principles of civil disobedience are followed:* "If we were to deny to every person who has engaged in . . . nonviolent civil disobedience . . . the right to enter a licensed profession, we would deprive the community of the services of many highly qualified persons of the highest moral courage" (*Hallinan v. Committee of Bar Examiners of State Bar,* 1966, p. 239).

A profound decision that confronts each of us is whether to, in essence, take the law into our own hands or to affirm Edmund Burke's (1790/1961) axiom: "One of the first motives to civil society, and which becomes one of its fundamental rules, is, that no man should be judge in his own cause" (p. 71). "Neither stance may seem acceptable to psychologists who believe that compliance with a legal or professional obligation would be harmful, unjust, or otherwise wrong. Absolute compliance connotes a 'just following orders' mentality all too ready to sacrifice personal values and client welfare to an imperfect system of rules and regulations. Selective noncompliance connotes an association of people who have anointed themselves as somehow above the law, able to pick and choose which legal obligations and recognized standards they will obey" (Pope & Bajt, 1988, p. 828).

As Pope and Bajt note, civil disobedience (Gandhi, 1948; King, 1958, 1964; Plato, 1956a, 1956b; Thoreau, 1849/1960; Tolstoy, 1894/1951) is useful in many contexts for resolving this dilemma. The individual breaks a law considered to be unjust and harmful but does so openly, inviting the legal penalty both to demonstrate respect for the system of law and to call society's attention to the supposedly unjust law. Counselors and therapists, however, often find this avenue of openness unavailable because of the requirement of confidentiality (see Chapter Twelve). If we, as a profession and as individual practitioners, are to address the possible conflicts between the law and the welfare of our clients, one of the initial steps is to engage in frequent, open, and honest discussion of the issue. The topic must be addressed in our graduate courses, internship programs, case conferences, professional conventions, and informal discussions with our colleagues.

The various mechanisms by which psychotherapists and counselors are held accountable for their actions can be a source of confusion for our clients, who often lack adequate information about these mechanisms. They may, for example, incorrectly believe that a professional ethics committee has the authority to revoke a license or that a licensing board has the power to expel a practitioner from a professional organization such as the American Psychological Association. The following sectors describe the four major mechanisms of accountability.

Professional Ethics Committees

Professional associations of therapists and counselors are voluntary organizations; membership is not a state or federal requirement for the practice of the profession. One can, for example, be licensed (by the state) and practice as a psychologist without being a member of the American Psychological Association (APA) or any other association. An association, through its ethics committee, holds its members accountable to the ethical principles it sets forth in the code it has developed. To illustrate how such a code is developed, we will focus on the American Psychological Association, which currently has about 65,000 members and fellows.

Founded in 1892 and incorporated in 1925, the APA first formed a Committee on Scientific and Professional Ethics in 1938. As complaints were brought to its attention, this committee improvised solutions on a private, informal basis. There was no formal or explicit set of ethical standards, so all of the committee's work was, of necessity, done on the basis of consensus and persuasion.

One year later, the committee was charged with determining whether a formal code of ethics would be useful for the organization. In 1947, the committee decided that a formal code of ethics would indeed be useful, stating "The present unwritten code is tenuous, elusive, and unsatisfactory" ("A Little Recent History," 1952, p. 425). The board of directors established a Committee on Ethical Standards to determine what methods to use in drafting the code. Chaired by Edward Tolman, the committee included John Flanagan, Edwin Ghiselli, Nicholas Hobbs, Helen Sargent, and Lloyd Yepsen (Hobbs, 1948).

Some members strongly opposed the development of an explicit set of ethical standards, and many of their arguments appeared in *American Psychologist*. Calvin Hall (1952), for example, wrote that any code, no matter how well formulated, "plays into the hands of crooks. . . . The crooked operator reads the code to see how much he can get away with, and since any code is bound to be filled with ambiguities and omissions, he can rationalize his unethical conduct by pointing to the code and saying, 'See, it doesn't tell me I can't do this,' or 'I can interpret this to mean what I want it to mean' " (p. 430). Hall endorsed accountability, but he believed that it could be enforced without an elaborate code. He recommended that the application form for APA membership contain this statement: "As a psychologist, I agree to conduct myself professionally according to the common rules of decency, with the understanding that if a jury of my peers decides that I have violated these rules, I may be expelled from the association" (pp. 430–431). Hall placed most of the responsibility upon graduate schools. He recommended that "graduate departments of psychology, who have the power to decide who shall become psychologists, should exercise this power in such a manner as to preclude the necessity for a code of ethics" (p. 431).

The Committee on Ethical Standards determined that because empirical research was a primary method of psychology, the code itself should be based upon such research and should draw upon the experience of APA members. As Hobbs (1948, p. 84) wrote, the method would produce "a code of ethics truly indigenous to psychology, a code that could be lived." The board of directors accepted this recommendation and a new committee was appointed to conduct the research and draft the code. Chaired by Nicholas Hobbs, the new committee included Stuart Cook, Harold Edgerton, Leonard Ferguson, Morris Krugman, Helen Sargent, Donald Super, and Lloyd Yepsen (APA Committee on Ethical Standards for Psychology, 1949).

In 1948, all 7,500 members of the APA were sent a letter asking each member "to share his experiences in solving ethical problems by describing the specific circumstances in which someone made a decision that was ethically critical" (APA Committee on Ethical Standards for Psychology, 1949, p. 17). The committee received reports of over 1,000 critical incidents. During the next years, the incidents with their accompanying comments were carefully analyzed, categorized, and developed into a draft code.

The emergent standards, along with the illustrative critical incidents, were published in *American Psychologist* (APA Committee on Ethical Standards for Psychology, 1951a, 1951b, 1951c). The standards were grouped into six major sections:

1. Ethical standards and public responsibility
2. Ethical standards in professional relationships
3. Ethical standards in client relationships

4. Ethical standards in research
5. Ethical standards in writing and publishing
6. Ethical standards in teaching

The draft generated considerable discussion and was revised several times. Finally, in 1953, it was formally adopted as the *Ethical Standards of Psychologists*.

In 1954, information on the complaints that the committee had handled for the past dozen years (during most of which there had been no formal code of ethics) was published in *American Psychologist* ("Cases and Inquiries," 1954). During this period, the ethical principles most frequently violated were:

*   Invalid presentation of professional qualifications (cited forty-four times)
*   Immature and inconsiderate professional relations (twenty-three)
*   Unprofessional advertisement or announcement (twenty-two)
*   Unwarranted claims for tests or service offered usually by mail (twenty-two)
*   Irresponsible public communication (six)

The most recent version of the ethical principles (American Psychological Association, 1990a) includes ten sections: responsibility, competence, moral and legal standards, public statements, confidentiality, welfare of the consumer, professional relationships, assessment techniques, research with human participants, and care and use of animals.

The most recent multiyear study of ethical complaints received by APA covered five years (Ethics Committee of the American Psychological Association, 1988b). The most frequent violations involved:

*   23 percent: Principle 6a (dual relationships including sexual intimacies with clients)
*   16 percent: Principle 3d (violating various APA standards and guidelines related to practice and research or governmental laws and institutional regulations)

- 8 percent: Principle 3c (acting in a way that violates or diminishes the legal or civil rights of others)
- 4 percent: Principle 5a (failing to preserve appropriate confidentiality of information concerning clients, students, and others)

Licensing and Certification

Each of the fifty states has its own set of administrative laws and regulations setting forth criteria for obtaining authorization to practice as (or, in some states, to identify oneself as) a psychotherapist or counselor. The states also set forth administrative standards of practice to ensure the safety and well-being of clients. In some cases, these administrative standards may embody ethical principles but not always. (For example, some may set forth the relatively mundane obligation to pay an annual licensing fee.) Formal licensing actions are how therapists and counselors are held accountable to these standards of practice. Violation of these standards may lead to the suspension or revocation of the practitioner's license or certification.

The data reviewed here concerning licensing disciplinary actions were collected by the American Association of State Psychology Boards (AASPB). The data are abstracted from the AASPB Disciplinary Data Reports from January 16, 1986 through July 1, 1988.

For at least two major reasons, the percentages that follow provide only the roughest estimations of the causes of disciplinary actions. First, as Dr. Pat Bricklin, AASPB president in 1988, stressed in authorizing the presentation of these percentage data, certain paths toward resolution of licensing complaints — for example, a licensee may unilaterally surrender a license to evade formal action by the board — may not be represented in the reports (Pat Bricklin, personal communication, September 8, 1988). Second, different states categorize the basis of disciplinary actions in different ways, some of them more vague than others ("ethical violations" or "unprofessional conduct," for example). We counted each disciplinary action only once; when more than one cause of action was given, we tried to select the most salient or informative basis. Although not all states indicated whether a dual relationship was sexual in nature, it was clear that most dual relationship violations involved sexual intimacies.

The disciplinary actions taken by licensing boards were based on violations in the following areas:

- 36 percent: Dual relationships (includes sexual intimacies with clients)
- 11 percent: Unprofessional conduct
- 10 percent: Conviction of a felony
- 8 percent: Failure to comply with board order
- 8 percent: Improper billing practices
- 6 percent: Incompetent manner of practice
- 3 percent: Mental incompetence
- 3 percent: Crime involving falsified Medicaid claims
- 3 percent: Fraud in application for license
- 2 percent: Disciplinary action in another jurisdiction
- 2 percent: Ethical violations
- 2 percent: Basis of violation not reported
- 1 percent: Violations of confidentiality
- 1 percent: Misrepresentation of competence
- 1 percent: Child abuse
- 1 percent: Failure to report child abuse

Malpractice

Each state has its own legislation and accumulated case law setting forth professional standards; violation of them can serve as the basis of malpractice suits against psychotherapists and counselors. Because the states differ in their legal standards, an act that one state may require may violate the legal standards in another state. In addition, some clinicians who work in federal institutions, such as Veterans Administration Medical Centers, may be subject to federal standards.

What are the primary reasons clinicians are sued? The data we review here, which are provided by the Insurance Trust of the American Psychological Association, include all 779 cases from February 1976 through May 1988 that have been closed. The twenty-seven major causes (indicated in italics) are listed in descending order of percentage of costs.

1. *Sexual Impropriety.* This category accounts for a dismaying 53.2 percent of the costs of malpractice cases and for 20.4 percent of the total number of claims. Dual relationships, particularly sexual dual relationships, account for the largest share of formal complaints against psychologists, whether those complaints are filed with the civil courts, licensing boards, or ethics committees. It is especially appalling to note that a sizable number of patients who are sexually victimized by their therapists are minors, some as young as three years old (see Chapter Nine). Sexual improprieties can occur not only between psychologists and their patients but also between psychologists and their students or supervisees (see Chapter Fourteen).

2. *Suicide of Patient.* Patients taking their own lives account for 11.2 percent of the total costs and about 5.8 percent of the total number of cases (see Chapter Thirteen).

3. *Incorrect Treatment.* Incompetence in the choice or implementation of the treatment plan accounts for about 8.4 percent of the total costs and about 13.2 percent of the total claims against psychologists. As noted earlier, incompetence is about the sixth most frequent cause of licensing disciplinary actions.

To a great degree, these cases may frequently be understood as psychologists undertaking work in areas for which they are not qualified by education, training, and experience (see Chapter Five). First, there are cases in which psychologists seek to change specialties—for example, from clinical to industrial-organizational or from experimental to counseling—without undertaking adequate formal education in the new specialty. It is important for APA members to be aware of the two policy statements regarding what is often called "retreading."

At its January 23–25, 1976, meeting, the APA Council of Representatives formally adopted the following "Policy on Training for Psychologists Wishing to Change Their Specialty." (Note particularly items 4 and 5.)

1. We strongly urge Psychology Departments currently engaged in doctoral training to offer training for individuals, already holding the doctoral degree in psychology, who wish to change their specialty. Such programs should be individualized, since background and career objectives vary greatly. It is desirable that financial assistance be made available to students in such programs.

2. Programs engaging in such training should declare so publicly and include a statement to that effect as a formal part of their program description and/or their application for accreditation.

3. Psychologists seeking to change their specialty should take training in a program of the highest quality, and, where appropriate, exemplified by the doctoral training programs and internships accredited by the APA.

4. With respect to subject matter and professional skills, psychologists taking such training must meet all requirements of doctoral training in the new specialty, being given due credit for relevant course work or requirements they have previously satisfied.

5. It must be stressed, however, that merely taking an internship or acquiring experience in a practicum setting is not, for example, considered adequate preparation for becoming a clinical, counseling, or school psychologist when prior training had not been in the relevant area.

6. Upon fulfillment of all formal requirements of such training program, the students should be awarded a certificate indicating the successful completion of preparation in the particular specialty, thus according them due recognition for their additional education and experience.

7. This policy statement shall be incorporated in the guidelines of the Committee on Accreditation so that

appropriate sanctions can be brought to bear on university and internship training programs which violate paragraphs 4 and/or 5 of the above.

In reaffirming and extending its previous policy, the APA
Council, at its January 22–24, 1982, meeting, adopted the following policy: "The American Psychological Association holds
that respecialization education and training for psychologists possessing the doctoral degree should be conducted by those academic units in regionally accredited universities and professional
schools currently offering doctoral training in the relevant specialty, and in conjunction with regularly organized internship
agencies where appropriate. Respecialization for purposes of
offering services in clinical, counseling, or school psychology
should be linked to relevant APA approved programs."

In addition to ensuring that they meet the education and
training standards for functioning within their specialty area,
clinical and counseling (as well as school and industrial-organizational) psychologists can benefit from carefully reviewing the
relevant *Specialty Guidelines* (APA, 1981) for their particular
specialty.

Second, there are cases in which psychologists, while functioning within their legitimate specialty area (for example, clinical or counseling), attempt to work with specific populations
(rape victims, incest perpetrators, the chronically ill) or to use
specific techniques (hypnotism, biofeedback, implosive therapy)
for which they are inadequately prepared in terms of their education, training, and experience. Research indicates that approximately 25 percent of psychologists acknowledge providing services outside their areas of competence, at least on a rare
basis (Pope, Tabachnick & Keith-Spiegel, 1987).

4.   *Undetermined.* When these figures were compiled, the causes
     of actions for about 7.9 percent of the total costs and about
     1.5 percent of the total cases were undetermined.
5.   *Diagnosis: Failure to or Incorrect.* This category accounts for
     3.7 percent of the total costs and 5.4 percent of the total

claims. (For discussion of diagnostic and assessment issues, see Chapter Eight.)

6. *Loss from Evaluation.* Individual claims to have suffered a
   loss as a result of an improper evaluation accounted for
   2.6 percent of the total costs and 8.5 percent of the total
   claims made against psychologists. Practitioners need to
   use exceptional care in assessing candidates for various
   positions — for example, high-stress jobs such as police
   work.

7. *Improper Death of Patient or Others.* This category accounts
   for 2 percent of the total costs and 3.2 percent of the total
   claims.

8. *Bodily Injury.* this category accounts for 1.6 percent of the
   total costs and 2.2 percent of the number of suits.

9. *Assault and Battery.* This cause of action accounts for 1.5
   percent of the total costs and 1.2 percent of the total claims.

10. *Countersuit for Fee Collection.* This category accounts for 1.3
    percent of the total costs and 6.2 percent of the total claims.

11. *Breach of Confidentiality or Privacy.* This category accounts
    for 1.3 percent of the total costs and 6.4 percent of the
    total claims in malpractice suits against psychologists. As
    noted previously, violations of confidentiality constitute
    the fourth most frequent cause of violations in ethics cases
    and the thirteenth most frequent cause of licensing disci-
    plinary actions. (For additional discussion of confidentiality
    issues, see Chapter Twelve.)

12. *Violation of Civil Rights.* This category accounts for 1.1 per-
    cent of the total costs and 2.1 percent of the total claims.
    A similar category constitutes, as noted earlier, the third
    most frequent basis of ethics cases in which there is a vio-
    lation.

13. *Miscellaneous.* This mysterious category accounts for 0.8
    percent of the total costs and 3.1 percent of the total claims.

14. *Defamation: libel/slander.* This category accounts for 0.7 per-
    cent of the total costs and 4.4 percent of the total claims.
    The average cost per claim of the thirty-four reported cases
    was only $4,680.

15. *Failure to Warn.* This cause of action accounted for 0.6 percent of the total costs and 0.4 percent of the total claims.
16. *Violation of Legal Regulations.* This category accounts for 0.5 percent of the total costs and 2.6 percent of the total suits filed against psychologists.
17. *Undue Influence.* This cause of action accounts for 0.4 percent of the total costs and 0.6 percent of the total claims filed against psychologists.
18. *Failure to Supervise Properly.* This category accounts for 0.3 percent of the total costs and 0.9 percent of the total claims filed. Independent practitioners need to stay aware that they are responsible for the services provided by psychological assistants or clinical supervisees who are working under their license.
19. *Loss of Child Custody or Visitation.* This category accounts for 0.2 percent of total costs and for 2.2 percent of the claims filed.
20. *Licensing or Peer Review.* This category accounts for 0.2 percent of the total costs and 2.1 percent of the total claims.
21. *Abandonment.* This cause of action accounts for 0.1 percent of the costs and 0.3 percent of the claims.
22. *Breach of Contract.* This cause of action accounts for 0.1 percent of total costs and 1.4 percent of total claims.
23. *Poor Results.* This category accounts for 0.1 percent of total costs and 1.7 percent of total claims.
24. *Premise Liability.* This category accounts for 0.1 percent of total costs and 2.4 percent of total claims.
25. *False Imprisonment/Arrest.* The eleven cases in this category average only $935 per case.
26. *Failure to Refer.* There was only one case, which cost $2,141.
27. *Failure to Treat.* There were only two cases, which averaged $38.

Criminal Behavior

Each state also has its own set of criminal laws, generally set forth in the penal code. Although we were unable to locate any reliable actuarial data concerning psychotherapists convicted of crimes, one of the most frequently mentioned areas involves fraud, particularly related to third-party billings. Donald Bersoff, then attorney representing the APA, emphasized the importance of conforming to all rules and regulations regarding billing practices for third-party coverage, both public and private, and noted that therapists currently serving time in prison could attest to the significance of violating those rules and regulations (see Ethics Committee of the American Psychological Association, 1988b).

Conclusion

Exceptional caution is appropriate in attempts to generalize, compare, or interpret the actuarial data presented in this chapter regarding complaints to ethics committees, licensing boards, and malpractice courts. Various types of actual violations, as the research indicates, may only very rarely lead to a formal complaint with a criminal court, civil court, licensing board, or ethics committee. Certain types of violation may be difficult to prove. Formal complaints may be informally resolved and thus not be reflected in archival data. And, as noted earlier, there are significantly different ways of classifying complaints.

Nevertheless, the general trends apparent in the data reviewed here may be useful to us. They can call our attention to aspects of our own practice in which there is room for improvement. They can also suggest possible topics for which we might want to take continuing education courses. These data, then, can provide a resource for us as individuals and as a helping profession seeking to maintain the high standards and integrity of our work and to minimize possible harm to those whom we serve.

Exceptional caution is also warranted in considering these mechanisms of accountability and their relationship to ethical behavior. All of us may experience some tendency to confuse at some level ethical behavior with that which does not bring us before one of these review agencies. Our sense of what is ethical runs through a reductionistic mill and becomes, in the worst-case scenario, "escaping detection" or "escaping account-ability." Much that we may do that is unethical may never come to light and may never trigger inquiry by one of these mechanisms of accountability. As noted in Chapter One, the principles articulated by our profession, by the licensing boards, and by the civil and criminal courts should not serve to inhibit careful ethical deliberation but more appropriately provide us with a framework and serve as a catalyst to provoke the painstaking ethical consideration of the situation that confronts us. The ethical deliberations of therapists and counselors often focus on the concepts of power, trust, and caring, the subjects of Chapter Three.

3

Trust, Power, and Caring

The ethical responsibilities of psychotherapists are founded upon the recognition that therapy involves trust, as well as power and caring.

Trust

Societies grant therapists professional status in acknowledgment of the fiduciary relationship between therapist and client. The social order expects or requires therapists not to exploit the trust with which it invests them and their enterprise; the social order depends on independent therapists to fulfill the trust for the benefit of individual clients as well as for the social order. (Many ethical dilemmas result when the benefit of the individual client is in actual or apparent conflict with the benefit of the social order or when the benefit of the client is in actual or apparent conflict with the benefit of those therapists who wish to assume the benefits but not the costs or responsibilities of the professional role.) In return for assuming a role in which the safety, welfare, and ultimate benefit of clients is to be held as a "sacred trust," therapists are entitled to the privileges and power due professionals.

This concept of trust is crucial for understanding the context in which clients approach and enter into a working relationship with psychotherapists. Clients rightfully expect or at least desperately hope that their trust in the therapist is not misplaced. Many, if not most, clients have deep fears that their trust may be betrayed. In some cases, these clients have often struggled painfully with issues of trust. In other cases, clients may be unaware of how their concerns about the trustworthiness of others have affected their ability to love, work, and enjoy life; the issues of trust may emerge gradually during the course of therapy. For each individual client, the issue of trust is not a conceptual abstraction of the type suggested by philosophical discussions of "fiduciary relationships" established to preserve and benefit the "social order." Trust is a deeply personal experience that defines the therapist-client relationship and provides a context for a sometimes bewildering diversity of hopes, hurts, failures, realizations, vulnerabilities, questions, and possibilities of change that can constitute the process of psychotherapy.

Power

The trust bestowed upon the psychotherapist by society and by individual clients is a source of power — for example, the power to assume and to attempt to fulfill or to manipulate, exploit, and betray the trust. But it is also a recognition of the many levels of power inherent in the role of therapist. The manifestations of the therapist's power range from the superficial to the profound, from temporary to enduring.

There is power inherent in the states' establishment of licensure as a requirement. Licensed professionals are permitted to engage in certain activities that are prohibited to others who do not possess the license. With the consent of patients, surgeons can cut human beings wide open and remove internal organs, anesthesiologists can render them unconscious, and psychiatrists can administer mind- or mood-altering drugs to them, all with the legal approval and authority vested by the state. Individuals will disrobe and willingly (well, somewhat willingly) submit to all manner of indignities when undergoing a comprehensive medical examination; they will allow the licensed physician to do things to them that no one else would be permitted to do. In a similar manner, clients will open up to a therapist, will allow the therapist to explore extremely private aspects of the client's history, fantasy life, hopes, and fears. Therapists are allowed by clients to hear the most personal secrets, material shared with literally no one else. Therapists are allowed to make inquiries that might provoke a slap in the face if asked by anyone else.

The states recognize the importance of protecting clients against the intentional or unintentional misuse of this power to invade the privacy of the person. (Metaphorically, psychotherapy, like surgery, is an "invasive procedure," although in both cases the client or patient consents to the invasion.) Except in a very few instances, most involving some sort of likely danger to a third party, therapists are required to keep confidential what they have learned about their clients through the professional relationship. The client's freely given informed consent must be obtained before a therapist can reveal confidential information to third parties. The fact that therapists hold such private information about their clients gives them considerable power in relation to their clients.

In licensing therapists, the states also invest them with the power of state-recognized authority to influence drastically the lives of their clients. Therapists are given the power to make decisions (though subject to judicial review) regarding the civil liberties of their clients. Some therapists are given the power to determine whether an American citizen constitutes an immediate danger to the life of another individual and therefore should be held against his or her will in an institution for observation or treatment. Alan Stone (1978), professor of law and medicine at Harvard University and a former president of the American Psychiatric Association, points out that the United States has incarcerated more of its citizens against their will for mental health purposes than any other country, that this process reached its peak in the 1950s when 1 out of every 300 citizens was held involuntarily in a mental institution, and that the abuse of this power has led to extensive reforms and formal safeguards.

Therapists also possess state-recognized authority to influence the lives of their clients through their testimony as experts in the civil and criminal courts and through similar judicial or administrative proceedings. Testimony by a therapist may determine whether someone convicted of murder will receive the death penalty or will be paroled. Testimony by a therapist may influence whether a parent is granted custody or visiting rights to his or her child. Testimony by a therapist may influence a jury in deciding whether a defendant was capable of committing a crime, was likely to have committed it, was legally sane at the time the crime was committed, or is likely to commit similar crimes in the future. Testimony by a therapist may also influence a jury to believe that a very young child was sexually molested or that the child fantasized the event (or was coached to make a false allegation as part of a custody dispute). And testimony by expert witnesses in personal injury suits may lead a jury to believe that the plaintiff is an innocent victim of a needless trauma who is suffering severe and chronic harm or that the same plaintiff is a chronic liar, a gold-digger, or a malingerer who is feigning or at least exaggerating dramatic symptoms.

The role of psychotherapist involves power beyond what a license establishes. There is power derived from knowledge. Psychotherapists formally study human behavior and the factors that influence motivation, decision, and action. They learn methods for promoting change. Acknowledgment and respect for this aspect of power is essential to avoid the subtle ways in which it may be used to manipulate and exploit clients.

The process of psychotherapy itself elicits, creates, and uses forms of power. Virtually all therapies recognize the importance of the client's expectation that the therapist's interventions will be able to induce beneficial change. One aspect of this expectation is sometimes termed the placebo effect, a factor that must be taken into account when conducting research into the possible efficacy of various interventions. Thus the client's investment of the therapist with power to occasion change can become a significant facet and resource of the change process itself.

The therapist frequently becomes invested with other important meanings as well. In the process termed *transference*, clients transfer feelings, attachments, or styles of relationship associated with figures from their past (such as parents) onto the therapist. The client may react toward the therapist as if he or she were the client's mother or father. Deep feelings such as love, rejection, shame, guilt, longing for approval, dependence, panic, and neediness — each perhaps representing the unfinished business of development or traumatic experiences needing understanding and healing — originally experienced within an early formative relationship may emerge in the therapist-client relationship in ways that tend to shock and overwhelm the client. Therapists' potential to elicit such profound feelings — simply by serving as a therapist — and to "feel" to the client as if the therapist were a figure from the client's past (with the client frequently functioning as if he or she were at an earlier stage of development) represent the sometimes surprising aspects of therapists' power to affect their clients.

In some approaches, the therapist may be active in establishing specific forms of power. For example, a family therapist may assertively "unbalance" the equilibrium and alliances among family members. A behavior therapist may create a hospital ward or halfway house in which "desirable" behaviors bring forth a rewarding response from the staff (perhaps in the form of tokens that can be exchanged for goods or privileges) and "undesirable" behaviors bring forth an aversive response; the power of the therapist and staff is used to control, or at least influence, the client's behavior.

The power differential is inherent in psychotherapy. Although certain approaches to therapy have emphasized egalitarian ideals in which therapist and client are "equal," such goals are viewed only within a narrowly limited context of the relationship. In truly equal relationships, in which there is no appreciable power differential, there is no designation of one member as "therapist" in relation to the other member, there is no fee charged by one member to the other for the relationship (nor are bills submitted to third parties such as insurance companies for reimbursement), there is no designation of the activity as "professional" (and thus falling within the scope of a professional liability policy), there is no use by one member of a license

to work with the other, and so on. A defining attribute of the
professional is the recognition, understanding, and careful handling of the considerable power inherent in the role.

Caring

Both the individual client and society recognize the diverse powers
of the professional role and place their trust in professionals to
use those powers to benefit — never to harm or exploit — those
who seek help from the therapist. The trust that society and the
individual client give must be matched by the caring of the therapist. Only within a context of caring — specifically caring about
the client's well-being — are the therapist's professional status
and powers justified. Historically, charging high fees did not
create or define professional status, nor did spending long years
in training or reaching a high level of expertise. The central,
defining characteristic of the professional was an ethic of plac-
ing the client's welfare foremost and not allowing professional
judgment or services to be drawn off course by one's own needs.

The touchstone for the approaches discussed in this book
is caring for and about people whom professional interventions
are meant to serve. The concept of caring as we use it in this
book is not relegated to a passive, empty sentimentality. Rather,
caring involves a responsiveness to the legitimate needs of a client
and a recognition that the client must never be exploited or
abused (although the therapist's personal wants and needs might
seem to justify and both the therapist's powers and the client's
vulnerabilities might facilitate tempting forms of exploitation
and abuse). Caring also involves actively assuming the full array of professional responsibilities to act in ways that legitimately
benefit and do not needlessly endanger the client and a diligence
in carrying out these profesional duties.

The powers of the therapist must be governed by an ethic
of caring for those whom the therapist serves. Caring whether
their powers will ultimately benefit or harm their clients helps
therapists to maintain an awareness of the consequences, meanings, and implications of their acts and to assume appropriate
and realistic responsibility for those acts. Caring about what

happens to clients is one of the strongest foundations for the myriad formal rules and regulations that are society's attempt to hold the therapist accountable, but it also encourages therapists to look beyond those explicit generalities. The professional attitude of caring is incompatible with a goal of meeting the lowest possible standards, doing as little as possible to get by, or using explicit regulations to resist, obscure, and evade professional responsibilities.

    Although few of us would set as a goal "meeting the lowest possible standards," certain assumptions, which many of us have held at some time during our careers, about the nature of therapy and counseling seem to encourage neglect of our ethical responsibilities. These assumptions are discussed in Chapter Four.

4

Common Misperceptions
That Interfere
with Ethical Practice

Some beliefs about the nature of psychotherapy or ethics can, in their more extreme forms, make it more difficult for us to recognize and consider the ethical aspects of our work. Six of these beliefs are discussed in this chapter.

Psychotherapy as Scientific Technology

Many practitioners consider psychotherapy to be a science or at least a scientifically based technology (see, for example, Singer, 1980). One of the great strengths of those who develop psychotherapeutic theory and methods is their willingness to adopt a scientific approach to their work: to define their terms and concepts clearly, to formulate their hypotheses in such a way that they can be verified or contradicted, to avoid over-reliance upon appeals to tradition or authority, to disseminate their findings in peer-reviewed journals that enable their findings to be evaluated independently by disinterested professionals prior to any attempts to gain fame and fortune in the popular media, and to acknowledge explicitly competing theories and contradictory data. This eagerness—or at least willingness—to be guided by empirical data that are systematically, carefully, and objectively gathered and evaluated tends to distinguish scientifically based psychotherapy from such popular methods of helping people with their problems as astrology, past-life regression, and channeling.

The risk is that some therapists may believe that their interventions constitute a scientific technology that is "value free" so that ethical analysis is not generally applicable or useful. This belief takes many forms. Most commonly, neither scientific research nor the resulting technologies are held to be, in and of themselves, ethical or unethical. The discovery of atomic energy and the development of technologies for releasing the "power of the atom" are viewed as ethically neutral. The technologies can be used to send cancer into remission or to obliterate a city. By extension, both the research scientists and the technologists are functioning within an ethically neutral sphere as long as they are functioning as scientists and technologists. According to this view, only those who are choosing the uses to which the research findings and resultant technologies will be put are engaging in activities subject to ethical scrutiny.

By analogy, therapists are believed to be developing and providing technologies relevant to human experience and behavior. It is the individual client who must assume responsibility for seeking the benefits of this technology and attempting to gain use of it in particular ways for his or her life (for example, to attempt to alter one's sexual orientation). It would be presumptuous, authoritarian, and paternalistic for the therapist to nullify the client's freedom of choice and range of opportunities. In summary, the therapist only provides an array of ethically neutral human technologies; the client decides to seek a particular technology for a particular goal. According to this scientific approach, the client must bear the ethical responsibility for the uses to which the technology of psychotherapy is put; the therapist is merely a conduit for the technology.

Psychotherapy as Mystery

Some therapists may emphasize the miraculous nature of life itself, the mystery of human experience, and the ultimately impenetrable enigma of existence. For them, the psychotherapist's attempts to understand and intervene in a client's life must rest within, depend on, and gain meaning from some form of philosophical skepticism such as that resulting from the line of British empiricists (for example, Hume), religious faith that attempts to symbolize and articulate the mystery, existentialism that attempts to confront and wrest meaning from the absurdity of ontological principles, or some other framework that views all human endeavors (such as psychotherapy) as possible or meaningful only in their relationship to an outlook focusing on the ultimate mystery of human life and experience.

A great strength of many of these approaches to therapy is their high level of respect for the client. The client is someone who can never be understood completely and can never be pigeonholed or taken for granted. Such approaches recognize and value the uniqueness of each client. Any tendencies to reduce clients to the status of labels, jargon, or variables are resisted. The special worth of the individual is held as primary. Clients may view such therapists as more approachable. Such therapists may communicate more warmth and convey less of the stereotype of the cold scientist in the white lab coat.

The risk is that an *exclusive* focus on the mystery of life may preclude or discourage a careful examination of the therapist's behavior and its implications, of the degree to which the therapist is fulfilling the responsibilities of his or her role. If assertions are carelessly made that all life is unpredictable, then therapists may tend to decline any responsibility for the negative consequences of their behaviors (because the outcomes would be, within this framework, unpredictable).

In the most extreme cases, therapists may come to believe that their work is beyond understanding or accountability. The therapist can take at least implicit credit for anything positive that happens while attributing the negative outcomes to fate, chance, and forces beyond human understanding. The therapist may become the stereotype of a guru.

Psychotherapy as Business

For those therapists who charge money for their services (whether in the form of fees from clients and insurance coverage or of wages or salary from an employer), therapy is at least in part a business. Therapists attempt to determine how much their services are worth, how much therapists providing comparable services are earning, how much clients (or employing institutions) are willing or able to afford, and how much they, as therapists, need or want to earn.

Many therapists have begun to adopt practices from the world of business to increase their revenue. They may conduct ad campaigns, employ sophisticated billing and bill-collection procedures, and rely on the professional guidance of attorneys, accountants, public relations specialists, and business consultants. The degree to which the business aspects of providing psychotherapeutic services have become of increasing interest and importance to therapists is reflected in the increasing percentage of space in professional association newsletters and of programs at professional conventions devoted to this topic.

This explicit attention to the financial aspects of our profession is relatively new. Older volumes that presented and reviewed psychotherapy research tended to ignore the subject entirely, prompting one contributor to comment, "As a footnote, I would like to remark that if a Martian read the volumes reporting the first two psychotherapy conferences and if he read all the papers of this conference it would never occur to him that psychotherapy is something done for money. Either therapists believe money is not a worthwhile research variable or money is part of the new obscenity in which we talk more freely about sex but never mention money" (Colby, 1968, p. 539).

Similarly, Mintz (1971) once termed fees a "tabooed subject," suggesting that "a varied set of guidelines" concerning fee payment has "functioned to inhibit therapists from inquiring too closely into the financial side of psychotherapeutic practice and into the actual effects it may have on the therapeutic enterprise" (p. 837). The pendulum seems to have swung forcefully the other way, and the financial aspects of psychotherapy are now discussed much more openly.

A strength of this trend is that the actual nature of the therapeutic relationship is more clearly and candidly defined. Therapists who charge for their services are forced to forgo a phony pose of "someone who just wants to help." Therapists who would otherwise claim to be offering unconditional acceptance and positive regard must acknowledge that the therapeutic process is in fact conditional upon payment of a fee. Therapists find it more difficult to gloss over both their complex motives in functioning as psychotherapists and the multilayered nature of the therapeutic relationship. Acknowledging, working through, and integrating the therapist's motivations for functioning as a therapist are beneficial if not essential steps in establishing an authentic, or unhypocritical, professional status and in understanding the therapeutic relationship.

The risk is that an overly exclusive focus on psychotherapy as business may obscure or erode the professional nature and ethical principles of the endeavor. The complexities of a business enterprise become an absorbing world, and the sometimes intense pressure not only to survive but also to thrive in the competition for clients and their revenue can make serious attention to ethical aspects of the business seem an undesirable luxury, a distraction from the responsibilities of ensuring that the business flourishes, or a quaint but dangerous inability to face up to "the real world." Virtually anything — including ethical principles — that would interfere with the generation of profit is reflexively rejected. Good business principles may somehow come to replace good ethical principles. Especially when the source of highly valued revenue is an institution — for example, when an insurance company or governmental agency pays part or all of the fee for large populations of clients — individual therapists may come to accept whatever standards and procedures the institution imposes even when such acceptance seems to lead to actions that violate professional prerogatives and ethics. For example, a president of the American Psychiatric Association noted some of the business practices within his profession that seemed, at a minimum, to blur the commitment to attend to the clinical needs of the patient: "payments to increase the length of stay of patients in hospitals. . . . Fifty dollars for each admission. Fifty dollars if you talk a patient out of leaving the hospital. Fifty dollars if you interfere with a patient's leaving against medical advice" (Fink, 1989, p. 1101; for other examples, see Pope, 1990a).

The language of ethics may still be used but only in the service of business principles. Having an explicit ethics code or discussions about ethics may be viewed as good public relations, good employee motivators, the necessary evil of complying with the demands of external regulatory agencies — in brief, good business.

Ethics as Adherence to Legal and Administrative Standards

Similar to the increasing interest in business aspects is the increasing interest in the legal regulation of psychotherapists and psychotherapy. Over the past few decades, states have adopted licensing or certification requirements for an increasing number of disciplines that provide therapy or counseling. The administrative regulations specifying the requirements for obtaining and renewing a license, the scope of mandatory or prohibited professional activities, and the disciplinary procedures for therapists who violate the requirements are becoming increasingly complex. In addition to these licensing or certification regulations are statutory injunctions in the criminal, evidence, and related codes regarding such issues as privilege and mandatory reporting of certain information obtained during professional activities. Civil suits filed against therapists can, upon appeal, establish precedents of case law (which interprets and supplements legislation) that further serve to regulate the behavior of psychotherapists. Again, the increasing role that such legal regulation plays in the professional life of the psychotherapist is reflected in the growing attention paid to such matters in professional newsletters and conventions.

A benefit of such legal regulation of the psychotherapies is that it forces professionals to confront the issue of what is permissible and impermissible professional behavior. Therapists are participants in this legal process in such diverse roles as members of licensing boards and expert witnesses in civil suits helping the judge and jury to understand the prevailing standards of conduct. Therapists are discouraged from the tendency to consider themselves as beyond accountability or questioning because of their professional status or expertise (see Chapter Two).

A risk in the emphasis on legal standards is that adherence to minimal legal standards, which in some cases is finding ways around those standards, can become a substitute for ethical behavior. This trend has become increasingly prevalent in the political arena. A politician or political appointee holding a position of great public trust may face incontrovertible evidence that he or she engaged in behavior that betrayed that trust. When no other defense or justification is available, the individual will insist that nothing wrong was done because no law was broken. (Even such desperate defenses hit a snag when it turns out that a law was broken; in those cases the individual stresses that there was a "technical violation of the law.") Thus an overly exclusive focus upon legal standards can discourage ethical awareness and sensitivity. It is crucial to realize that ethical behavior is more than simply avoiding violation of legal standards and that one's ethical and legal duties may, in certain instances, be in conflict.

Ethics as Rare Dramatic Conflict

It is often the intensely dramatic ethical conflict that grabs headlines in the popular media and professional newsletters. The following hypothetical scenarios, both from the forensic setting, illustrate these vividly charged conflicts.

The client is a serial killer of numerous children. He has been convicted and sentenced to death. During all phases of the trial, he has claimed privilege and refused to let the therapist that he has recently seen disclose any of the therapeutic discussions. Only the therapist knows, based upon what the killer has told her, the names of many missing children whom her client killed and where their bodies are hidden. (All these disclosures came after the fact; the state had no legislation that required or permitted the therapist to disclose this information.) Parents of literally hundreds of missing children are desperate to find out whether their child was among the murdered and, if so, where they can recover the body. Should the therapist violate both the law and her agreement with the client by disclosing this information?

A therapist working in the prison system is assigned a prisoner who is on death row. The execution has been delayed because the prisoner has been evaluated as incompetent due to a mental disorder. The therapist, after the first two sessions, determines that the prisoner is suffering from an extreme stress reaction (understandable in light of the death sentence), which has elicited a psychosis. If the therapist's intervention is effective, the client will be put to death; if the therapist's intervention is ineffective, the client will live. What should the therapist do?

Such instances, when they are publicly reported, tend to galvanize intense interest and concern. They highlight both the inescapable ethical conflicts that clinical work entails as well as the profound consequences — sometimes a matter of life or death — of the ethical decisions that therapists make.

A possible risk, however, is that we may focus our ethical awareness and concern almost exclusively on such dramatic situations. As a result, we may overlook the numerous, less dramatic, but no less significant ethical decisions that each of us — no matter what our setting, clientele, or approach — faces in our day-to-day clinical work.

Ethics as Mindless Rule Following

In our graduate training, we are given sets of ethical standards or principles developed by the profession and are urged to take them to heart. We read them, discuss them, and try to think how we can put all the "do's and don't's" into practice.

Such codes are of enormous importance. They tell clinicians, clients, and the public what sorts of behaviors are and are not permissible, desirable, or mandatory. They help identify important areas of ethical concern. They set forth standards to which the professional agrees to be held accountable (see Chapter 2).

A risk is that we may come to view ethics as simply the obedient and unthinking following of a certain set of "do's and don't's." As we noted in the Preface and Chapter One, ethics codes, standards, or rules can never legitimately serve as a substitute for a thoughtful, creative, and conscientious approach to our work. They can never relieve us of the responsibility to struggle with competing demands, multiple perspectives, evolving situations, and the prospect of uncertain consequences — that is to say, life as it is lived, in all its complexity. The studies of how individuals respond to ethical dilemmas, how they decide what course to take, how they evaluate their own behavior and the behavior of others, and how they construe and make attributions regarding the outcomes demonstrate the complex interactions among the individual, the specific dilemma, formal and implicit values and principles, and the context (Brown, 1990; Gibbs & Schnell, 1985; Gilligan, 1982; Gilligan, Ward, Taylor & Bardige, 1988; Hamilton, Blumenfeld & Kushler, 1988; Kelman & Hamilton, 1989; Kohlberg, 1969; Lickona, 1976; Mednick, 1989; Milgram, 1974; Shaver & Drown, 1986; Smith & Whitehead, 1988). Ethics codes, standards, or rules serve best to awaken us to potential pitfalls but also to opportunities, to guide and inform our attempts to help without hurting. They cannot do our work for us.

If we — rather than lists of "do's and don't's" — have the responsibility for responding ethically to our clients — in a way that does justice to the power, trust, and caring inherent in our work — then we must possess at least a basic competence to perform our work. That competence is the subject of the next chapter.

5

Competence in Practice

When clients put their trust in us as professionals, one of their most fundamental expectations is that we will be competent. Society, through the courts and licensing boards, also holds us to this standard.

Clients, of course, may have a variety of unrealistic — sometimes virtually magical — expectations. They may hope, for example, that we will be able to assess and intervene with certainty and without error, that we will be able to guarantee results, and that we will be able to meet all of their needs. Unfortunately some clinicians may suffer from such delusions and may encourage these beliefs in their clients.

Although the omniscient, omnipotent, and error-free clinician is a myth, therapists and counselors have an ethical and legal responsibility to offer clients a basic and adequate competence. In psychotherapy and counseling, *competence* is complex and difficult to define. Licensing boards and the civil courts sometimes specify defining criteria for discrete areas of practice. More often, however, they tend to require simply that in whatever area of therapy and counseling the clinician is practicing, he or she should possess *demonstrable* competence. When demonstrable competence is formally and explicitly required, the clinician is prevented from merely asserting competence;

evidence of the competence must be produced. Generally, this evidence comes in the form of the clinician's formal education, professional training, and carefully supervised experience.

The competence requirement is frequently established in the ethical, legal, and professional standards governing the work of therapists. For example, article 8 ("Rules of Professional Conduct"), section 1396 of California Title 16 declares, "The psychologist shall not function outside his or her particular field or fields of competence as established by his or her education, training and experience." Section 1.6 of the *Specialty Guidelines for the Delivery of Services by Clinical Psychologists* (APA, 1981, p. 7) states, "Clinical psychologists limit their practice to their demonstrated areas of professional competence." Principle 2a of the APA's "Ethical Principles of Psychologists" (1990a, p. 391) states, "Psychologists accurately represent their competence, education, training and experience."

To affirm the crucial importance of competence as an ethical requirement is to recognize that the power (see Chapter Three) implicit and invested in the therapist's role cannot be handled in a careless, ignorant, thoughtless manner. The complex, hard-to-define nature of therapy may tend to obscure the reasonableness and necessity of this requirement. It becomes more vivid by analogy to other fields. A physician who is an internist or general practitioner may do excellent work, yet who among us would want that physician to perform coronary surgery or neurosurgery on us if the physician does not have adequate education, training, and supervised experience in these forms of surgery? A skilled professor of linguistics may have a solid grasp of a variety of Indo-European languages and dialects and yet be completely unable to translate a Swahili text.

Given the encouragement of clients who may hold exaggerated beliefs about our talents, it may be difficult for us to acknowledge that we simply are not competent to intervene in a particular situation. It may be particularly difficult if we do not want to disappoint or alienate a valued source of referrals who has referred a client to us or if we desperately need new clients to cover office overhead and feel that we cannot afford to turn away potential business. Nevertheless, extensive education, training, and supervised experience in working with adults does not qualify us to work with children, solid competence in providing individual counseling or psychotherapy does not qualify us to lead a therapy group, and expertise in working with individuals suffering from profound depression does not qualify us to work with individuals suffering from developmental disorders.

At times, the complexity of the situation requires exceptional care and skill in determining how to respond most effectively and ethically to a client's needs while remaining within one's areas of competence. For example, a counselor may begin working with a client on issues related to depression and bulimia, two areas in which the counselor has had considerable education, training, and supervised experience. But much later the therapeutic journey leads into a problem area—incest, for example—in which the counselor has no or very limited expertise. As another example, a client initiates psychotherapy to deal with what seem like moderately severe difficulties concentrating at work. Soon, however, it becomes apparent that the client is suffering from agoraphobia. Can the counselor ethically presume that the course on anxieties and phobias that he or she took ten years ago in graduate school is sufficient to address the problem competently? The counselor faces the decision whether there is time, energy, and commitment necessary for consultation to provide the most up-to-date treatment for agoraphobia or whether it will be necessary to refer the client to someone who is a specialist or at least competent to work with someone suffering from agoraphobia.

Clinicians who work in isolated or small communities may face this dilemma frequently. If the therapist or counselor is the only practitioner in an area, he or she probably will frequently encounter unfamiliar problems. Fulfilling the ethical responsibility of competence is especially difficult for these practitioners. They are constantly attending workshops and consulting long distance with a variety of experts to ensure that their clients are receiving competent care.

Despite the clear ethical and legal mandates to practice only with competence, therapists and counselors may suffer lapses. A national survey of psychologists, for example, found that almost one-fourth of the respondents indicated that they had practiced outside their area of competence either rarely or occasionally (Pope, Tabachnick & Keith-Spiegel, 1987).

To ensure that their services meet the ethical responsibility of competence, clinicians may wish to consider each of the five following aspects.

Certification and Licensure

In an effort to protect clients from incompetent practitioners, states have instituted a wide variety of laws that restrict counseling and psychotherapy to those who have met the criteria imposed by the state (see Chapter Two). Psychologists, social workers, and, more recently, mental health counselors, marriage and family therapists, and addiction counselors have sought credentialing in most states (Cummings, 1990). Therefore, to practice legally, counselors and therapists must obtain the appropriate credentials for the state or secure supervision according to the state's guidelines.

Two considerations are especially important in considering state licensure or certification as a potential indicator of competence. First, is there any research or evidence of any type that the licensing (or certification) examination or other criteria actually ensure general competence, protect consumers, or promote higher standards of practice? Thoughtful analyses have called the states' efforts into question (see, for example, Hogan, 1979; Ziskin, 1981). And do the states' oral or written tests for licensure meet the relevant criteria set forth by the American Psychological Association in the *Standards for Educational and Psychological Testing* (1985) or other formal guidelines regarding validity? Second, note that any general competence that may be assured by the licensure process does *not* mean that, for example, a person licensed as a psychologist is necessarily competent to perform all the tasks that a psychologist may, under the authority of the license, perform. For instance, a person may have been licensed as a psychologist and the state may authorize psychologists to conduct neuropsychological assessment, biofeedback, and hypnosis; a given individual, however, may be

licensed as a psychologist and have no competence whatsoever
in any of these three areas.

Standards and Guidelines

Standards and guidelines published by professional associations
provide information relevant to competent practice and frequently set forth explicit criteria for competence. Among the
publications distributed by the American Psychological Association, the following may be exceptionally useful in auditing our
own practice to ensure that we possess adequate competence
in each relevant area:

- *Ethical Principles of Psychologists* (APA, 1990a)
- *Casebook on Ethical Principles of Psychologists* (APA, 1987a)
- *General Guidelines for Providers of Psychological Services* (APA, 1987b)
- *Guidelines for Providers of Psychological Services to Ethnically and Culturally Diverse Populations* (APA, 1990b)
- *Standards for Educational and Psychological Testing* (1985)
- *Guidelines for Computer-Based Tests and Interpretation* (APA, 1986)
- *Ethical Principles in the Conduct of Research with Human Participants* (APA, 1982)
- *Guidelines for Conditions of Employment of Psychologists* (APA, 1987c)

It is useful to be familiar with the ethical and professional standards not only of psychologists but also of the other
major mental health professionals, such as those provided by
the American Association for Counseling and Development
(1988), American Association for Marriage and Family Therapy (1988), American College Personnel Association (1989),
American Psychiatric Association (1989), and National Association of Social Workers (1989; 1990).

Approaches, Strategies, and Techniques

A crucial aspect of competence is our ability to select approaches,
strategies, or techniques that show evidence or promise of effec-

tiveness in addressing the client's problem. If our methods are to avoid charlatanism, hucksterism, and well-meaning ineffectiveness, they must *work* (at least some of the time). Thus the supposed competence of the practitioner has little meaning if his or her methods lack competence. In his provocative article "The Scientific Basis of Psychotherapeutic Practice: A Question of Values and Ethics," Singer (1980) emphasized the importance of clinicians remaining knowledgeable concerning the emerging research basis of the methods they use. Weiner (1989) provides a case example: "A psychologist commenting on the assessment of alleged sexual abuse was heard to identify a 'certain sign': If a girl sees Card IV on the Rorschach as a tree upside down, then she has been a victim of sexual abuse. Whatever tortuous rationale might be advanced on behalf of such an influence, there is not a shred of empirical evidence to support it. Indeed, there is precious little evidence to support any isomorphic relationship between specific Rorschach responses and specific behavioral events. Psychologists who nevertheless use Rorschach responses in this way are behaving unethically, by virtue of being incompetent" (pp. 829–830).

Stress, Distress, and Dysfunction

The therapist's emotional health is seen as the sine qua non of adequate and ethical professional functioning in most theories of counseling and psychotherapy (Thoreson, Miller & Krauskopf, 1989). A goal of many training programs is to promote trainees' self-awareness and ability to recognize personal issues that could negatively affect the therapeutic process and harm the client. The Accreditation Committee of the American Psychological Association (1989) clearly requires a training faculty to be responsible for assessment and continual feedback to students—not only to improve skills but also to prevent individuals who are psychologically unsuited from entering the field.

Because some (*by no means all*) mental, emotional, or behavioral problems can affect the clinician's ability to function effectively, it is a fundamental ethical responsibility that the clinician monitor carefully any vulnerability to or emergence of such problems. Under no circumstances should a therapist use "personal problems" or similar rationales to excuse his or her unethical behavior.

What percentage of counselors and therapists report distress or impairment of the type that would interfere with providing safe and effective services? Various studies have reported a range of 2–10 percent (Boice & Myers, 1987; Bouhoutsos, 1983; Farber, 1985; Helman, Morrison & Abramowitz, 1987). However, higher percentages are occasionally reported. Thoreson, Miller, and Krauskopf (1989) reported a "distress band" of 9–19 percent; 19 percent reported distress in one problem category while 9 percent reported from two to four categories of distress. Pope, Tabachnick, and Keith-Spiegel (1987) found that over half (59.6 percent) of their national sample of clinical psychologists acknowledged having worked when too distressed to be effective.

What are the predominant sources of distress and impairment? Bouhoutsos (1983) reported survey responses from 581 licensed psychologists in California. The 6 percent who indicated that they had experienced problems during the past year that had diminished their ability to practice effectively reported problems related to alcohol and other substance abuse, major mental illness, major physical illness or disability, and grief over loss or separation from a loved one.

Thoreson, Miller, and Krauskopf (1989), in a survey of a state psychological association, found that members reported depression, marital dissatisfaction, feelings of loneliness, recurrent physical illness, and drinking problems.

Pope and his colleagues (1987) found that one out of every fifteen or twenty (5.7 percent) of their national sample of clinical psychologists reported that they had conducted therapy, at least on a rare basis, while under the influence of alcohol.

In Deutsch's (1985) survey of psychologists, social workers, and master's-level counselors in regard to perceived personal problems, the most frequently reported type of problem was relationship difficulty. More than half the sample reported difficulties with depression; 11 percent reported difficulties with substance abuse; 2 percent had attempted suicide. Deutsch also surveyed treatment-seeking behaviors. While a quarter of the sample sought therapy for their difficulties, many reported a reluctance to seek therapy based on lack of resources, fear of exposure, concern about confidentiality, and fear of professional censure.

Deutsch's findings indicating such reluctance on the part of so many psychotherapists to seek help are ironic and disturbing given that our livelihood as therapists and counselors depends on others' willingness to take that risk. Moreover, many people consider personal therapy a critical component in the training and maintenance of competence. It is very difficult to understand what it means to be a client unless we have been in that role ourselves. Therapists who completed their training and began practicing without undertaking personal therapy have often been shocked when they eventually did start therapy. Suddenly they understood much more immediately, effectively, and personally what their own clients had been going through. What it means to contact a therapist to request help, to show up for a first appointment, to discuss very private matters, to react seemingly irrationally to the therapist's vacations and unanticipated absences, to wonder about the therapist's personal life, and to worry about confidentiality, are very difficult to imagine accurately if we have not "been there" ourselves. Moreover, the experience of psychotherapy can help enhance clinical ability by improving empathy and self-awareness, resolving personal conflicts, and providing a useful learning experience by observing an experienced therapist (Guy, Stark & Spolestra, 1988). The development of such empathy may play a crucial role in our development as therapists (Sarason, 1985; Stoltenberg & Delworth, 1987).

The survey evidence suggests that most therapists seek therapy (Guy, Stark & Spolestra, 1988). However, Guy and his colleagues expressed concern that 22.9 percent of the participants in their survey of APA Divisions 12 (Clinical Psychology), 29 (Psychotherapy), and 42 (Independent Practice) had not received individual therapy. (The discrepancy in figures reported by Deutsch and by Guy and his colleagues may be due, at least in part, to questionnaire wording and sample selection.)

Functioning as therapists or counselors may itself be a source of considerable stress and distress for therapists. Farber (1985), for example, found that while most private practice psychologists were satisfied with their work, 2–6 percent felt greatly affected by work-induced stress, particularly when their work seemed to overemphasize cognitive components at the expense of affect and spontaneity. Research suggests that therapists who experience a client's suicide may be vulnerable to profound trauma (Goldstein & Buongiorno, 1984; Kleespies, Smith & Becker, 1990; Litman, 1965; see also Chapter Thirteen).

Peer Support and Review

All of us have blind spots and vulnerabilities. Our colleagues constitute a tremendous resource for helping us to avoid or correct mistakes, to identify stress or personal dilemmas that are becoming overwhelming, and to provide fresh ideas, new perspectives, and second and third opinions. A national survey of psychologists, in fact, found that therapists rated informal networks of colleagues as the most effective resource for prompting effective, appropriate, and ethical practice (Pope, Tabachnick & Keith-Spiegel, 1987). Informal networks were seen as more valuable in promoting ethical practice than laws, ethics committees, research, continuing education programs, or formal ethical principles.

The therapist's competence is useless for the patient unless the patient has adequate access to it. Chapter Six explores the issue of access as reflected in the beginning and termination of the therapeutic relationship and in the planned and unanticipated absences of the therapist.

6

Beginnings and Endings, Absences and Accessibility

A fundamental responsibility of the psychotherapist is to clarify the boundaries of the relationship. Two of the most important boundaries are the beginning and ending of the therapy. The individual seeking help needs to know whether he or she is a client and whether he or she can reasonably expect that a particular clinician will act to fulfill the responsibilities of the role of therapist.

Therapists must be alert to possible complications and confusions. An individual may call for an initial appointment. The therapist may assume that the session is one of initial evaluation regarding possible courses of action (for example, if therapy makes sense for the individual, or what modality of therapy under what conditions implemented by what clinician seems most promising). The individual, however, may assume that the clinician, by virtue of accepting that request for an initial appointment, has become his or her therapist. Similarly, several months into treatment a client may become enraged at the therapist but be unable to express that anger directly. The client may leave suddenly halfway through a session and miss the regular appointment time for the next five weeks, during which the client fails to return any of the therapist's phone calls. Is that client still a client or has a de facto termination occurred?

Acting to prevent unnecessary misunderstandings regarding the beginning and ending of therapy is part of a clinician's more general ethical responsibility to make clear the availability of and access to therapeutic resources. One of the more immediate aspects of this responsibility is for both therapist and client to understand clearly when and under what circumstances the therapist will be available for sessions or for phone communication and what resources will be available for the client when the therapist is not available.

Clarification is important for a variety of reasons. First, it forces the therapist to consider carefully this client's needs for phone access during the course of therapy. For example, is this an impulsive, depressed client with few friends who might need phone contact with the therapist or some other professional in the middle of the night to avert a suicide? Clarification enables the therapist to plan for such contingencies.

Second, by leading the therapist to specify backup availability — for example, what the client can do if unable to reach the therapist by phone in an emergency — the efforts to clarify availability enable the therapist to prepare for therapeutic needs that are difficult or impossible to anticipate. For example, a client with moderate coping resources may attend appointments regularly over the course of a year or two, never contacting the therapist between sessions. However, during a period when the therapist is seriously ill and unavailable for any professional activities, the client may receive numerous shocks, such as the loss of a job or the death of a child, that may activate pathologies that had not emerged during treatment. The client may become acutely suicidal and need prompt access to therapeutic resources. Careful planning by the therapist may meet such needs that are virtually impossible to anticipate with a specific client.

Third, explicit clarification of the client's access to the therapist or to other therapeutic resources encourages the therapist to think carefully about the effects that the therapist's availability and unavailability are likely to have upon the client and upon the course of treatment. For example, some clients are likely to experience overwhelming feelings of sadness, anger, or abandonment when the therapist goes on vacation. Other clients may find the clear boundaries that the therapist has established so uncomfortable and infuriating that they are constantly "testing" both the therapist and the boundaries. Such clients may frequently show up at the therapist's office at the wrong time for their appointment, may leave urgently cryptic messages ("Am quitting therapy; no hope; life too painful; can't go on") on the therapist's answering machine without leaving a number where they can be reached, and may persistently try to discover the therapist's home address and home phone (if the therapist customarily keeps these private).

Fourth, when therapist and client work together to develop a plan for emergencies during which the therapist might not be immediately available, the process can help the patient to acknowledge realistically his or her dependence and needs for help and to assume — to the extent that he or she is able — realistic responsibility for self-care during crises. For example, the therapist may ask the client to locate the nearest hospital providing twenty-four-hour services and to develop ways of reaching the hospital in an emergency. As the client assumes responsibility for this phase of crisis planning, he or she increases the sense of self-efficacy and self-reliance (within a realistic context), becomes less inclined to view therapy as a passive process (in which the therapist does all the "work"), and may feel less panicky and helpless when facing an impending crisis or the therapist's future absences.

Fifth, the process of clarification encourages the therapist to consider carefully his or her own needs for time off, for time away from the immediate responsibilities of work. Such planning helps ensure that the therapist does not become overwhelmed by the demands of work and does not experience burnout. The drawing of such boundaries also encourages the therapist to attend explicitly to other sources of meaning, joy, fulfillment, and support so that he or she does not begin looking to clients to fill personal needs.

What follow are some of the major areas of accessibility that the therapist needs to clarify in a manner consistent with his or her own needs and style of practice and with the clinical needs of each client.

Therapy Sessions

Some clinicians hold to exact time boundaries. With virtually no exceptions, they begin and end the session "on the dot." Even if the client has just experienced a painful breakthrough and is in obvious distress, the therapy session is not extended. In some situations, ending promptly is a practical necessity: The therapist may have another client scheduled to begin a session immediately. In other situations, observing strict time boundaries is required by the theoretical orientation; running over the time boundary might be considered by the therapist to constitute a breaking of the "frame" of therapy or represent the therapist and client colluding in acting out.

Therapists must consider carefully the approach to time boundaries of the session that best fits their own theoretical orientation and personal needs. The effects of the policy upon individual clients needs to be considered, and the client should understand the policy.

Therapist Availability Between Sessions

When and under what conditions can the client normally speak with the therapist between sessions? Some therapists receive nonemergency calls from clients during reasonable hours (for example, 9:00 A.M. to 9:00 P.M.) of weekdays when they are not otherwise engaged. A very few therapists take nonemergency calls when they are conducting psychotherapy. We recommend against this practice, which seems disrespectful of the client who is in session and seems to have numerous potentially harmful effects upon the course of therapy of the client whose session is interrupted by nonemergency calls (or who is aware that any session might be interrupted at any time by such calls to the therapist).

The therapist needs to be clear about the times between sessions when he or she can be contacted on a nonemergency basis. For example, are weekend calls or calls on holidays such as Labor Day, Memorial Day, or Martin Luther King Day acceptable?

An extremely important point to clarify is whether the therapist will speak with the client more than briefly by phone when there is no emergency. Some clients may wish to use phone calls to address the unresolved issues form the last therapy session, to share a dream while it is still "fresh," or to talk over how to handle a situation at work. Some therapists may see such ad hoc phone sessions as therapeutically useful for some clients. The sessions may, for example, help particularly fragile and needy clients, who might otherwise require day treatment or periodic hospitalizations, to function under the constraints of once or twice weekly outpatient therapy. They may help some clients to learn how to use and generalize the adaptive skills they are acquiring in office sessions; the phone sessions serve as a bridge between office therapy sessions and independent functioning by the client.

Some therapists, however, believe that such phone sessions during which therapy is conducted are — except under rare emergency conditions — countertherapeutic. For example, such therapists might view extended phone contacts between sessions as similar in nature and effect to going beyond the temporal boundary at the end of a session.

Again, whether the therapist uses an approach that includes therapy sessions conducted by phone on an ad hoc basis or prohibits them is less important than that: (1) the therapist think through the issues carefully in terms of consistency with the theoretical orientation, (2) the therapist consider carefully the implications of the policy for the individual client, and (3) that both therapist and client clearly understand what the ground rules are.

Vacations and Other Anticipated Absences

As mentioned earlier, and as readily recognized by almost anyone who has been a therapy client, extended and sometimes even very brief interruptions in the schedule of appointments can evoke deep and sometimes puzzling or even overwhelming reactions in a client. What is important is that the therapist give the client adequate notice of the anticipated absence. If the therapist tends to take a two-week vacation at the same time each year, there may be no reason for the therapist to omit this information from the customary orientation provided to a new client. If the therapist finds that he or she will be taking a six-week sea cruise during the coming year, the therapist should consider carefully if there is any compelling clinical reason to withhold this information from the client as soon as the therapist decides to take the cruise. Prompt notification of anticipated therapist absences minimizes the likelihood that the client will experience a psychologically paralyzing traumatic shock, gives the client maximal time to mobilize the resources to cope with the therapist's absence in a way that promotes independence and growth, and enables the client to become aware of reactions and to work with them during the sessions before and after the absence.

Serious Illness and Other Unanticipated Absences

Both therapists and clients tend to find comforting the fantasy that the therapist is essentially invulnerable. Therapists may enjoy the feeling of strength and of being a perfect caregiver that such a fantasy, which sometimes occurs on an unconscious level, provides. Clients may soothe themselves (and avoid confronting some personal issues) with the fantasy that they are being cared for by an omnipotent, immortal parental figure.

However, as distressing as it may be to acknowledge, especially on the day-to-day basis of the practice of psychotherapy, therapists may experience strokes, heart attacks, or other serious medical conditions with sudden onset. They may suffer from Alzheimer's disease, AIDS, or cancer. They may, while driving with caution, be involved in a car wreck. They may come down with a case of food poisoning. They may take a hard fall, leaving them in a coma. They may be stabbed, shot, or beaten during the commission of a crime. They may be called away suddenly to cope with a family emergency. Or, relatively less pernicious, they may come down with a bad case of the flu, confining them to bed for a week or two. These scenarios are not simply the common fantasies of patients experiencing deep negative transference. They represent the possibilities in store for any human, including therapists.

Just as the breadwinners of a family try to take such contingencies into account in planning for their family's welfare, responsible therapists need to take into account these distressing possibilities and to develop reasonable procedures so that the unanticipated absence (whether temporary or permanent) of the therapist will not unduly undermine the client's welfare. Each therapist will create his or her own way of approaching this issue. The approach must be suited to the personal and professional resources of the therapist, the nature and style of the practice, the theoretical orientation and treatment modality, and, of course, the specific needs of individual clients. Among the questions to which therapists must develop practical answers are these:

1. If the therapist is incapacitated, who will notify the clients? Will there be clear procedures for informing clients in advance of their next appointment? There should be a clear list—easily accessible to whoever is responsible for notifying the clients—indicating scheduled appointments and phone numbers or addresses for contacting clients. It may not be practical to go through all client files in an effort to figure out who is a current client, when their next appointment is, and what their current phone and address are. The pocket or briefcase schedule books that many therapists keep with them may be difficult (or impossible) for a colleague to locate during a crisis, and many such books would require deciphering skills beyond the abilities of all but the most advanced cryptographers. Providing adequate arrangements for unanticipated absences during which the therapist is incapacitated is a particularly difficult challenge for solo private practitioners who employ no support staff. The method developed for notifying clients must take into account the client's legal and ethical right to confidentiality.

2. Is there an individual whom clients, subsequent treating therapists, and others can easily contact to ask about the condition and course of recovery of the temporarily incapacitated therapist?

3. If the therapist is unable to attend to any professional responsibilities, how are the therapist's records handled?

Who, if anyone, gains legitimate access to the records? Who, if anyone, has proper authority to act on behalf of the therapist and send copies of the records to subsequent treating therapists or to others whom the client authorizes to receive the records? The records of treatment-to-date may gain exceptional importance because clients may be at increased risk for crisis if their therapist has suddenly become unavailable.

Steps for Fostering Availability of Help in a Crisis

Once the client clearly understands how he or she can contact the therapist by phone between regularly scheduled appointments, the therapist and client can discuss appropriate arrangements for situations in which this phone system is inadequate. The client, for example, may experience an unanticipated crisis and be unable to reach the therapist promptly by phone because the therapist's line is busy for an extended time, the therapist's answering service mishandles the client's call, the therapist is in session with another client who is in crisis, or any number of other typical or once-in-a-lifetime delays, glitches, or human errors. For the five reasons cited at the beginning of this chapter, planning for such "unanticipated" breakdowns in communication can enable access to prompt clinical services in time of crisis and can foster more careful therapeutic planning.

If the client's need for help is urgent and if the therapist is unavailable, is there a colleague who is providing coverage for the therapist? The decision of whether to arrange for coverage for a specific client is complex. Perhaps the first question that must be addressed is what sorts of information will the covering clinician be provided about the client? Will the coverage provider receive a complete review and periodic update of the client's clinical status, treatment plan, and therapeutic progress? Will the coverage provider have access to the client's chart? Will the coverage provider keep a separate set of notes regarding information supplied by the primary therapist? To what extent will the coverage provider need to secure independent informed consent for treatment by the client? The more foreseeable or the greater the risk that the client will experience a serious crisis demanding prompt intervention, the more compelling the reason for the primary therapist to brief the coverage provider in a careful, thorough manner.

Once the therapist has determined what degree of coverage seems necessary or appropriate for a specific client, a second question to consider is how would introducing the possibility of or actually implementing such coverage affect the client's status or treatment dynamics? Some clients might feel greatly reassured to know that the therapist is taking his or her responsibilities seriously and is thinking through carefully possible, even if unlikely, treatment needs. Other clients may become alarmed and feel as if the therapist were predicting that a crisis would occur. Still other clients may stall in their progress; the strict privacy and confidentiality of therapy is essential for them, and the knowledge that the therapist would be sharing the contents of sessions with the coverage provider would inhibit the client's ability to explore certain issues or feelings. In many cases, discussion between the therapist and client of the question of whether specific coverage will be provided is useful therapeutically.

If it is decided that specific coverage will be provided, a third question for the therapist to consider is what will best ensure the client's right to adequate informed consent for sharing information with the coverage provider and otherwise making arrangements for the coverage?

A fourth question involves the selection of a clinician to provide the coverage. The primary therapist may incur legal (that is, malpractice) liability for negligence in selecting the coverage. If, for example, the clinician providing the coverage mishandles a crisis situation or otherwise harms the client through inappropriate acts or failures to act, the primary therapist may be held accountable for failure to screen and select an appropriate clinician. However, the ethical and clinical issues are much more subtle. It is important to select a clinician who is well trained to provide the type of care that the client may need. The primary therapist may be tempted to select a clinician solely (and perhaps inappropriately) upon grounds of expedience. The primary therapist may know that the clinician is really not a very good clinician and is perhaps less than scrupulous in his or her professional attitudes and actions. Furthermore, the primary therapist may be aware that the clinician does not tend to work effectively with the general client population that the therapist treats. Nevertheless, the therapist may push such uncomfortable knowledge out of awareness because this particular clinician is handy, and it might take considerable effort to locate an appropriate and trustworthy coverage provider. As in so many other situations discussed in this book, the Golden Rule seems salient. If we were the patient, or if it were our parent, spouse, or child who desperately needed help in a crisis when the primary therapist is unavailable, if the careful handling of the crisis were potentially a matter of life and death, what level of care would we believe adequate in selecting a clinician to provide the coverage? If, for example, our parent became suddenly despondent, received a totally inadequate response from the clinician providing the coverage, and committed suicide, would convenience seem sufficient rationale for the primary therapist's selection of that clinician to provide the coverage?

If (for clinical or other compelling reasons) no clinician has been identified to provide coverage or if the identified clinician is for some reason unavailable, to whom does the client in crisis turn when the primary therapist is unavailable? It may be useful for the client to locate a psychiatric hospital, a general hospital with psychiatric services, or other facility providing emergency psychiatric services. There are at least four crucial aspects of accessibility of such services. First, is the facility nearby? Are the services available on a twenty-four-hour basis? (That is, if the crisis occurs in the middle of the night, on a weekend, or on a holiday, will the client find help available?) Second, can the client afford to use the facility? Some facilities charge exceptionally high prices and may offer services only to those who can provide proof of ability to pay—for example, an insurance policy currently in effect. Third, does the client know where the facility is located and what its phone number is? Especially during a crisis, even basic information (such as the name of a hospital) may be hard to remember. In some instances where both the therapist and client believe that there is a high risk for a crisis, it may be useful for the client to write down the name of the hospital, the address, and the phone number to carry with him or her and to leave by the phone at home. Sometimes close friends or family play a vital role in supporting a client in times of crisis. If the circumstances are appropriate, the client may also wish to give this information to a close friend or relative. Fourth, both the therapist and client need to have justifiable confidence that the facility provides adequate care. Substandard care may aggravate a crisis; in certain instances no care from certain facilities may be better than an inappropriate response.

If the primary therapist, secondary coverage, and designated facility are all unavailable — for whatever reason — in time of crisis, is there an appropriate hotline or other twenty-four-hour phone service that can provide at least an immediate first-aid response to the crisis and attempt to help the client locate a currently available source of professional help? Some locales have twenty-four-hour suicide hot lines. There may be a twenty-four-hour crisis line providing help for individuals with certain kinds of problems. At a minimum, such a phone service may help a client to survive a crisis. For some clients (for example, those who cannot afford a phone at their residence), identifying locations of phones that will be accessible in times of crisis will be an important part of the planning.

If all the previously mentioned resources are inaccessible to the client, the client may nevertheless be able to dial 911, the operator, or a similar general call for emergency response. The client may then be guided to sources of help or, if appropriate, an ambulance or other emergency response may be dispatched.

Whenever a therapist is assessing a client's resources for coping with a crisis that threatens to endanger or overwhelm the client, it is important to evaluate not only the professional resources but also the client's social resources. Individual friends and family members may play key roles in helping a client to avert or to survive a crisis (though a friend or family member can also initiate, intensify, or prolong a crisis). In some instances, nonprofessional groups, such as Alcoholics Anonymous, may provide virtually twenty-four-hour access to support. The presence of such social supports gains in relative importance when the client's access to professional help tends to be difficult. For example, some clients (especially those who cannot afford a phone) cannot gain easy access to a phone (particularly if they arc experiencing a crisis in the middle of the night). For many clients, the awareness of such social supports helps them to feel less isolated and thus less vulnerable to becoming overwhelmed by a crisis.

Conclusion

Awareness — particularly a careful, imaginative awareness — plays a fundamental role in ensuring that clients have adequate access to the help they need, particularly in times of crisis when the therapist is not immediately available. In hospital and similar organizational settings, the apparent abundance of staff may lead to a diffusion of responsibility in which no one is actually available to help a patient in crisis. Levenson and Pope (1981), for example, present a case study in which a psychology intern was assigned responsibility to contact promptly a suicidal individual who had been referred to the outpatient unit by the crisis service and to arrange for conducting an intake assessment. The intern, however, was absent from the staff meeting at which the assignment was made. His supervisor, also absent from the meeting, had sent him to attend a two-day training session at another institution. During the next few days, the individual committed suicide.

The hospital's thanatology committee concluded that the crisis service had handled the situation appropriately in referring to the outpatient unit. The outpatient unit itself was not involved in the postmortem investigation because, according to the hospital's procedures, outpatient cases are not opened until the potential patient is contacted by the outpatient unit for an intake screening. The intern himself struggled with his reactions to these events. Among his conclusions was that he had "at some level internalized the organizational view that no one is really responsible" (p. 485).

Imagination is useful in creating an awareness of the types of crises the client might experience and what difficulties he or she might experience in trying to gain timely access to needed resources.

Thinking things through on a "worst possible case" basis can help the therapist to anticipate the ways in which Murphy's Law can make itself felt in human endeavors. No therapist is infallible. The most careful and confident assessment of a patient's potential for crisis can go awry for any number of reasons. But the therapist should take into account his or her own fallibility and plan for the unexpected.

Similarly, imaginative approaches can create accessibility to needed resources. For example, a therapist was treating an extremely isolated, anxious, and troubled young woman pro bono because of the client's lack of money. From time to time the client became overwhelmed by anxiety and was acutely suicidal. However, she had no practical access to hospitalization because of her own financial status and the absence in the community of sufficient beds for those who lacked adequate funds or insurance coverage. In similar cases, the therapist had encouraged clients to make arrangements to have a trusted friend come by to stay with the client during periods of extreme dysfunction and suicidal risk. However, this client was so socially isolated that she had no friends, and the therapist was unable to locate an individual—from local church and synagogue groups or from hospital volunteer organizations—who could stay with the client in times of crisis. Determined to come up with some arrangement that would help ensure the client's safety and welfare should the client experience a crisis and the therapist be unavailable, the therapist and client finally hit upon the possibility of the client going to the local hospital's waiting room. (The waiting room adjacent to the emergency room was open round the clock.) The therapist contacted hospital personnel to make sure that they would have no objection to her client showing up at odd hours to sit for indefinite periods of time in the waiting room.

The arrangement worked well during the remaining course of therapy. According to the client, simply knowing that there was someplace for her to go frequently helped her to avoid becoming completely overwhelmed by external events or by her own feelings. On those occasions when she did feel herself to be in crisis and at risk for taking her own life, she found that going to the hospital waiting room seemed helpful; it made her feel more active and aware that she was doing something for herself. Being out of her rather depressing and claustrophobic apartment, sitting in a "clean, well-lighted place," and being around other people (who, because they were strangers, would be unlikely to make, in her words, "demands" on her) were all factors that helped her feel better. Knowing that there were health care professionals nearby (even though she had no contact with them) who could intervene should her impulses to take her own life become too much for her, and aware that she was carrying out a "treatment plan" that she and her therapist had developed together helped her to feel more calm, less isolated, and comforted in her time of crisis. The waiting room strategy enabled this highly suicidal client to be treated safely, although hospitalization was not feasible, during the initial period of therapy when outpatient treatment alone seemed, in the judgment of both the therapist and an independent consultant, inadequate and when the client could not afford additional resources. It made imaginative use of resources that were readily available in the community and were accessible to the client.

Understanding the degree to which individual clinicians and mental health organizations will be accessible and will make help available is a crucial aspect of the patient's informed consent, the focus of the following chapter.

7

Informed Consent
and Informed Refusal

Nothing blocks a patient's access to help with such cruel efficiency as a bungled attempt at informed consent. We may have struggled successfully with the challenges outlined in the previous chapter. The doors to our offices and clinics are open wide. The resources are all in place. But not even the most persistent patients can make their way past our intimidating forms (which clerks may shove at patients when they first arrive), our set speeches full of noninformative information, and our nervous attempts to meet externally imposed legalistic requirements. A first step in remedying the situation is to recognize that informed consent is not a static ritual but a useful process.

The Process of Informed Consent

The process of informed consent provides both the patient and therapist with an opportunity to make sure that they adequately understand their shared venture. It is a process of communication and clarification. Does the therapist possess at least a sufficient initial understanding of why the patient is seeking help? Does the therapist know what the patient expects, or hopes, or fears from the assessment and therapy? Does the patient adequately understand the approach the clinician will be using to assess and address the problem? Does the patient know the common effects of using such an approach and alternative approaches to his or her problem?

Informed consent also involves making decisions. The patient must decide whether to undertake this course of assessment and treatment, whether to begin immediately or to delay, and whether to try an alternative approach or an alternative therapist. The therapist must decide whether the patient is competent to exercise informed consent (very young children may not be capable of providing fully informed consent) and whether the situation may justify an intervention in the absence of fully informed consent (the patient is threatening to kill his or her spouse and is, in the therapist's judgment, likely to do so). The therapist must also consider whether a fully competent patient has been provided the relevant information with which to make a decision and sufficiently understands that information and whether the patient is providing consent on an adequately voluntary basis.

Finally, informed consent tends to be a recurrent process. The patient may consent to an initial psychological, neuropsychological, and medical assessment as well as to a course of individual psychotherapy based upon an initial, very provisional treatment plan. Several months into treatment, the treatment plan may be significantly altered on the basis of the results of the assessments, the patient's diverse reactions to various components of the treatment plan, and the patient's changing needs. As the treatment plan undergoes significant evolution, the patient must adequately understand these changes and voluntarily agree to them.

The Basis of Informed Consent

Informed consent is an attempt to ensure that the trust required of the patient is truly justified, that the power of the therapist is not abused intentionally or inadvertently, and that the caring of the therapist is expressed in ways that the patient clearly understands and desires. Case law has provided a clear analysis of the basis and workings of informed consent. Much of this case law has concerned medical practice, but the relevance (not always complete) of the principles to clinical assessment and psychotherapy can be inferred.

Historically, the health care professions took a fairly arrogant and authoritarian position in regard to what the patient needed. Informed consent is a principle absent from the Hippocratic Oath. It was simply assumed that the doctor knew what was best. The patient obviously did not have sufficient training and knowledge, let alone objectivity, to determine what procedures were indicated.

A landmark in the shift away from this authoritarian approach appeared in a New York case. In 1914, Judge Benjamin Cordozo, who later became a justice of the U.S. Supreme Court, wrote that "every human being of adult years and sound mind has a right to determine what shall be done with his own body" (*Schloendorf v. Society of New York Hospital*, 1914, p. 93). It was not so much that this case changed the customary procedures by which doctors went about their work; it was more that Judge Cordozo articulated clearly the principle that it was the patient — rather than the doctor — who had the right to decide whether to undertake a specific treatment approach. The implications of this principle lay dormant for decades.

A second landmark appeared in 1960, in the Kansas case of *Natanson v. Kline*. The court reaffirmed the Cordozo principle: "Anglo-American law starts with the premise of thorough-going self-determination. It follows that each man is considered to be master of his own body" (p. 1104). The court stated that to make this determination, the patient obviously needed the relevant information. But what information was relevant was left entirely to the community of doctors to decide: "The duty . . . to disclose . . . is limited to those disclosures which a reasonable . . . practitioner would make under the same or similar circumstances. . . . So long as the disclosure is sufficient to assure an informed consent, the physician's choice of plausible courses should not be called into question if it appears, all circumstances considered, that the physician was motivated only by the patient's best therapeutic interests and he proceeded as competent medical men would have done in a similar situation" (1960, p. 1106). This case exemplifies the "community standard" rule: Informed consent procedures must adhere only to what the general community of doctors customarily do.

In 1972, with decisions handed down by the Federal District Court in Washington, D.C., and the California Supreme Court, the full implications of Judge Cardozo's principle were realized. The reasoning began with the reaffirmation of *Schloendorf v. Society of New York Hospital* and an emphasis that the patient must have relevant information that only the doctor can provide: "The root premise is the concept, fundamental in American jurisprudence, that '[e]very human being of adult years and sound mind has a right to determine what shall be done with his own body. . . .' True consent to what happens to one's self is the informed exercise of a choice, and that entails an opportunity to evaluate knowledgeably the options available and the risks attendant upon each. The average patient has little or no understanding of the medical arts, and ordinarily has only his physician to whom he can look for enlightenment with which to reach an intelligent decision. From these almost axiomatic considerations springs the need, and in turn the requirement, of a reasonable divulgence by physician to patient to make such a decision possible" (*Canterbury v. Spence*, 1972, p. 780).

It is thus the patient, and not the doctor, who must make the final decision, and this decision, to be meaningful, must be based on an adequate range of information to be provided by the doctor: "[I]t is the prerogative of the patient, not the physician, to determine for himself the direction in which he believes his interests lie. To enable the patient to chart his course knowledgeably, reasonable familiarity with the therapeutic alternatives and their hazards becomes essential" (*Cobbs v. Grant*, 1972, p. 514).

This line of reasoning emphasized the exceptional trust and dependence inherent in health care, differentiating them from the milder versions of trust and dependence — often dealt with using a caveat emptor principle — characteristic of less intense, less intimate transactions in the marketplace: "A reasonable revelation in these aspects is not only a necessity but, as we see it, is as much a matter of the physician's duty. It is a duty to warn of the dangers lurking in the proposed treatment, and that is surely a facet of due care. It is, too, a duty to impart information which the patient has every right to expect. The patient's reliance upon the physician is a trust of the kind which traditionally has exacted obligations beyond those associated with arms-length transactions. His dependence upon the physician for information affecting his well-being, in terms of contemplated treatment, is well-nigh abject" (*Canterbury v. Spence,* 1972, p. 782).

This landmark case law specifically rejected the idea that doctors, through their "community standards," could determine what degree of information the patient should or should not have. It was not up to doctors, individually or collectively, to decide what rights a patient should have in regard to informed consent or to determine those rights indirectly by establishing "customary" standards regarding what information was and was not to be provided. Patients were held to have a right to make an informed decision and the courts were to guarantee that they had the relevant information for making the decision. The court observed, "We do not agree that the patient's cause of action is dependent upon the existence and nonperformance of a relevant professional tradition. . . . Respect for the patient's right of self-determination on particular therapy demands a standard set by law for physicians rather than one which physicians may or may not impose upon themselves" (*Canterbury v. Spence,* 1972, pp. 783–784).

The case law clearly states the need for doctors to provide adequate relevant information regardless of whether the patient actively asked the "right" questions in each area. Thus doctors were prevented from withholding or neglecting to provide relevant information because a patient did not inquire. The doctors were seen as having an affirmative duty to make an adequately full disclosure:

> We discard the thought that the patient should ask for information before the physician is required to disclose. Caveat emptor is not the norm for the consumer of medical services. Duty to disclose is more than a call to speak merely on the patient's request, or merely to answer the patient's questions: it is a duty to volunteer, if necessary, the information the patient needs for intelligent decision. The patient may be ignorant, confused, overawed by the physi-

cian or frightened by the hospital, or even ashamed to inquire. . . . Perhaps relatively few patients could in any
event identify the relevant questions in the absence of prior
explanation by the physician. Physicians and hospitals have
patients of widely divergent socio-economic backgrounds,
and a rule which presumes a degree of sophistication which
many members of society lack is likely to breed gross ine-
qualities [*Canterbury v. Spence,* 1972, p. 783].

Realizing that some patients would certainly choose not
to undertake specific assessment or treatment procedures, the
courts emphasized that understanding what might happen as
a result of *not* getting adequate assessment or treatment was as
relevant to making an informed decision as understanding the
assessment and treatment procedures themselves. Thus the
California Supreme Court, in 1980, not only reaffirmed the principles previously set forth in *Canterbury v. Spence* and *Cobbs v.
Grant* but also affirmed that patients have a right to informed
refusal of treatment as well as a right to informed consent to treatment: "The rule applies whether the procedure involves treatment
or a diagnostic test. . . . If a patient indicates that he or she is
going to *decline* a risk-free test or treatment, then the doctor has the
additional duty of advising of all the material risks of which a reasonable person would want to be informed before deciding not to
undergo the procedure. On the other hand, if the recommended
test or treatment is itself risky, then the physician should always
explain the potential consequences of declining to follow the recommended course of action" (*Truman v. Thomas,* 1980, p. 312).
Recognizing that some doctors might be intimidated by
the daunting thought of presenting to patients essentially all they
had learned during their training and that patients might be
ill-suited recipients of jargon-filled lectures, the court emphasized that the patient needed only the relevant information to
make an informed decision but needed it in clear, straightfor-
ward language: "The patient's interest in information does not
extend to a lengthy polysyllabic discourse on all possible complications. A mini-course in medical science is not required"
(*Cobbs v. Grant,* 1972, p. 515).

In summary, the courts, in the 1970s, tended to shift the locus of decision making clearly to the patient and the responsibility for ensuring that the decision was based upon adequate, relevant information clearly to the doctor. The California Supreme Court attempted to articulate the basis of this concept of informed consent:

> We employ several postulates. The first is that patients are generally persons unlearned in the medical sciences and therefore, except in rare cases, courts may safely assume the knowledge of patient and physician are not in parity. The second is that a person of adult years and in sound mind has the right, in the exercise of control over his own body, to determine whether or not to submit to lawful medical treatment. The third is that the patient's consent to treatment, to be effective, must be an informed consent. And the fourth is that the patient, being unlearned in medical sciences, has an abject dependence upon and trust in his physician for the information upon which he relies during the decisional process, thus raising an obligation in the physician that transcends arm-length transactions. From the foregoing axiomatic ingredients emerges a necessity, and a resultant requirement, for divulgence by the physician to his patient of all information relevant to a meaningful decisional process [*Cobbs v. Grant,* 1972, p. 513].

These principles have begun to pass from case law into legislation. Indiana's House Enrolled Act of 1984, for example, stated, "All patients or clients are entitled to be informed of the nature of treatment or habilitation program proposed, the known effects of receiving and of not receiving such treatment or habilitation, and alternative treatment or habilitation programs, if any. An adult voluntary patient or client, if not adjudicated incompetent, is entitled to refuse to submit to treatment or to a habilitation program and is entitled to be informed of this right" (Section F).

Considerations in Fulfilling
Informed Consent Responsibilities

No unvarying and inflexible method exists for legitimately ensuring a client's informed consent. No method can relieve us of a thoughtful response to the particulars before us. All of us have developed unique and personal styles as therapists or counselors. Each of our clients is unique.

Informed consent is a recurrent process — not a static set of pro forma gestures — that develops out of the relationship between clinician and client. It must fit the situation and the setting. It must respond not only to the explicit standards of the clinician's professional associations, such as the American Psychological Association, but also to the relevant state and federal laws and to the evolving case law. It must be sensitive to the client's ability to understand — is the client a young child, developmentally disabled, suffering from severe thought disorder? — the relevant information, and the client's situation — is the client in the midst of a crisis, referred for mandatory treatment by the courts, being held against his or her will in a mental hospital? Human sensitivity and professional judgment are required.

As we attempt to create and sustain the process of informed consent, several considerations, noted in the remainder of this chapter, are useful.

Failing to Provide Informed Consent. In considering how we are to meet the client's right to informed consent, we must remain aware that that right is violated, perhaps frequently. We can take those instances to justify our own decisions not to accord clients informed consent, or we can use those instances as an opportunity to consider the matter from the client's perspective. How would we feel if we were the clients who had been kept in the dark, who had not been given the chance to make a decision on an informed basis?

One of the most egregious examples of the withholding of informed consent involved the provision of free medical care to hundreds of U.S. citizens (J. H. Jones, 1981; see also Rivers,

Schuman, Simpson & Olansky, 1953; U.S. Public Health Service, 1973). The program began in 1932 and continued to 1972. If all we were told was that the government (through what eventually became the U.S. Public Health Service) was giving us comprehensive medical care, how would we likely feel? Grateful? Relieved that we would be spared financial burdens? Excited that we would have access to state-of-the-science medical interventions provided by the federal government? Who among us would turn down this rare opportunity?

What the participants were not told is that they were being used to research the effects of syphilis when it goes untreated. Treatment for syphilis was in fact withheld from all the individuals. Research procedures were presented as treatment; for example, painful spinal taps were described to the subjects as a special medical treatment. Although Public Health Service officials denied that there were any racist aspects to this research, admission to the program was limited to male African-Americans.

More recent examples are numerous. Hospitals, for example, may perform AIDS tests on virtually all patients without patients' knowledge or permission, sometimes in direct violation of state law (Pope & Morin, 1990). As another example, Stevens (1990) described a testing center that administered the Stanford-Binet Intelligence Scale so that students could be placed in the appropriate classes at school. The information schools received contradicted that given to the child's parents. In one case, for example, the report sent to the school "recommended that David be placed in a class for average students"; the report sent to the parents recommended that "David should be placed in a class for superior students" (p. 15). Here is how the testing center explained the policy: "The [report] we send to the school is accurate. The report for the parents is more soothing and positive" (p. 15).

How would we feel if we relied on the government and health care professions to provide us with free medical care when in fact they were observing the untreated consequences of a painful, virulent, usually fatal disease? How would we feel if we went to a hospital for help and were given an AIDS test without our knowledge or permission? How would we feel if we were given completely inaccurate information about the results of an intelligence assessment because someone else thought it would be "more soothing"?

Benefits of Informed Consent. Approaching the issue of informed consent, we may, as clinicians, fear that providing adequate information to clients and explicitly obtaining their consent will somehow derail therapy and may, in fact, have detrimental consequences for our clients. The research has not supported these fears. The process of informed consent tends to be beneficial. A variety of studies have indicated that the use of informed consent procedures makes it more likely that clients will become less anxious, follow the treatment plan, recover more quickly, and be more alert to unintended negative consequences of the treatment (Handler, 1990).

Unequal Opportunity for Informed Consent. It is crucial that we do not accord unequal opportunities to our clients for informed consent based upon prejudice and stereotypes (see Chapter Eleven). Research suggests that this unfortunately happens, at least occasionally, thus depriving some clients of their right to informed consent. For example, in an examination of informed consent practices, Benson (1984) found that whether important information was disclosed by a sample of physicians was systematically related to such factors as the patient's race and socioeconomic status.

Cognitive Processes. Clinicians must maintain a current knowledge of the evolving research and theory regarding the cognitive processes by which people arrive at decisions (see, for example, Bell, Raiffa & Tversky, 1989; Evans, 1989; Goleman, 1985; Janis, 1982; Kahneman, Slovic & Tversky, 1982; Langer, 1989; Rachlin, 1989). This research and theory can help clinicians to understand the factors that influence clients who are choosing whether to participate in assessment or treatment procedures.

At a Harvard University hospital, Barbara McNeil and her colleagues (1982) presented individuals with two options, based upon actuarial data concerning patients suffering from lung cancer. The actuarial data indicated whether patients had chosen a surgical or a radiological treatment for their cancer and what the outcome had been. Of those who chose surgery, 10 percent died during the operation itself, an additional 22 percent died within the first year after the surgery, and another 34 percent died within five years. Of those who chose radiation therapy, none died during the radiation treatments, 23 percent died within the first year, and an additional 55 percent died by the end of five years.

If you were given those actuarial data, which intervention would you choose? When these data were presented, 42 percent of the participants in the study indicated that they would choose radiation. Note that the data were presented in terms of mortality — the percentages of patients who died. When the same actuarial information was presented in terms of percentages of patients who survived at each stage — for radiation, 100 percent survived the treatment, 73 percent survived the first year, and 22 percent survived five years — only 25 percent chose radiation. The change from a mortality to a survivability presentation caused a change in the way individuals cognitively processed the information and arrived at a decision.

Because our interventions may have profound effects for our clients, and the decisions they may make regarding whether to begin therapy and what sort of therapeutic approaches to try are significant, we have an important ethical responsibility to attend carefully to the form in which we present information relevant to those decisions.

Problems with Forms. Many of us may be so eager to begin doing therapy that we do not feel inclined to make the effort to talk with our clients about the issues and information relevant to informed consent. We attempt to push all the responsibility off onto a set form, and we try to let the form do all the work. Those of us who work within clinics or hospitals may not even handle such forms. The client who shows up for an initial appointment may be handed an imposing looking form by the receptionist, asked to read it, sign it, and return it before seeing the therapist. The form itself may have been crafted by the clinic or hospital's attorney and may not even have been reviewed by a clinician. The wording may be in intimidating legalese and bureaucratic jargon. Such forms may be intended more to protect the organization against successful lawsuits than to enable the client to understand the options and to make reasonable decisions.

Providing information in written form can be vital in ensuring that clients have the information they need. But the form cannot be a substitute for an adequate process of informed consent. At a minimum, the clinician must discuss the information with the client and arrive at a professional judgment that the client has adequate understanding of the relevant information.

Clinicians using consent forms must ensure that their clients have the requisite reading skills. Illiteracy is a major problem in the United States; clinicians cannot simply assume that all of their clients can read. Moreover, some clients may not be well versed in English, perhaps having only rudimentary skills in spoken English as a second or third language.

Not only must the client be able to read but the form itself also must be readable. Grundner (1980, p. 900) noted that great effort has been made to ensure that "consent forms have valid content, but little effort has been made to ensure that the average person can read and understand them." He obtained five forms and analyzed them with two standardized readability tests. He found that "the readability of all five was approximately equivalent to that of material intended for upper division undergraduates or graduate students. Four of the five forms were written at the level of a scientific journal, and the fifth at the level of a specialized academic magazine" (p. 900).

Reading a form does not ensure that the client understands the material or can remember it even a short time later. Robinson and Merav (1976) reinterviewed twenty patients four to six months after they had read and signed a form for informed consent and had undergone treatment. They found that all patients showed poor recall regarding all aspects of the information covered by the form, including the diagnosis, potential complications, and alternate methods of management. Cassileth,

Zupkis, Sutton-Smith, and March (1980) found that only one day after reading and signing a form for informed consent, only 60 percent of the patients understood the purpose and nature of the procedures. A perfunctory indication from clients that they understand can be unreliable (Irwin et al., 1985). The clinician bears the responsibility for ensuring that the client actually understands the information. Determining the client's ability to understand as well as the degree to which he or she actually does understand relevant information is part of the larger task of assessment, the subject of the next chapter.

8

Assessment, Testing, and Diagnosis

Diagnosis, testing, and assessment can greatly affect our clients. Improper diagnoses can deprive clients of appropriate and effective treatment. Jobs and promotions may be unavailable, freedom from prisons or locked wards may be denied, and custody hearings may be lost, all on the basis of a test report.

Conducting assessments seems to be one of the more troublesome areas of practice for therapists and counselors, at least according to the insurance statistics. Rick Imbert (personal communication, April 18, 1988), president of the American Professional Agency, which provides professional liability coverage to APA members, notes that inadequate or inappropriate diagnosis, testing, and assessment are a major cause of successful malpractice suits against psychologists (see Chapter Two).

The picture is complicated by judicial pronouncements about the nature of certain diagnoses. For example, "an Arkansas appeals court ruled that bipolar disorder is a physical, not mental, illness and should be reimbursed at whatever payment rate an insurer has established for covering treatment of physical illness" ("Court Holds Bipolar," 1988, p. 1). By a four to three majority, the U.S. Supreme Court asserted that "even among many who consider alcohol a 'disease' to which its victims are genetically predisposed, the consumption of alcohol is not regarded as wholly involuntary" and refused to strike down a Veterans Administration regulation that characterized "primary alcoholism as a willfully incurred disability" rather than an uncontrollable disease (*McKelvey v. Turnage,* 1988; *Traynor v. Turnage,* 1988).

Any of us who practice independently rather than within institutional settings may face greater challenges in consistently performing evaluations that are ethical, accurate, useful, and consistent with the latest advances in research and theory. We tend to lack the "ready made" professional support, educational resources, and peer review characteristic of many clinics and hospitals with their inservice training programs, grand rounds, case conferences, and program evaluation. We may need to be more active in updating, improving, and monitoring our evaluation services.

The following considerations are useful in identifying ethical pitfalls and in helping to ensure that diagnosis, testing, and assessment are as valid and useful as possible for both clinician and client.

Awareness of Standards and Guidelines

The American Psychological Association publishes several documents relevant to testing, assessment, and diagnosis (see Chapter Two). Reviewing them on a periodic basis can help ensure that work in this area meets the highest standards. The most relevant documents include *Standards for Educational and Psychological Testing* (1985), *Guidelines for Computer-Based Tests and Interpretations* (APA, 1986), and the "Ethical Principles of Psychologists" (APA, 1990a). Principle 8 of the *Ethical Principles* is entitled "Assessment Techniques" and has six specific subprinciples. The *Casebook on Ethical Principles of Psychologists* (APA, 1987a) presents vignettes illustrating common violations of Principle 8.

Staying Within Areas of Competence

A psychology degree from a particular program, a specific internship experience, and a license to practice psychology do not, in and of themselves, qualify a professional to administer, score, interpret, or otherwise use psychological tests (see Chapter Five).

Hall and Hare-Mustin (1983, p. 718) reported an APA ethics case in which "one psychologist charged another with incompetence, especially in testing. . . . CSPEC (Committee on Scientific and Professional Ethics and Conduct) [Authors' note: CSPEC was the former name of the APA Ethics Committee] reviewed the report of the state committee, which had carried out the investigation, and found that the person had no training or education in principles of psychological testing but was routinely engaged in evaluations of children in child custody battles. The committee found violation of Principle 2a, competence in testing, and stipulated that the member should work under the supervision of a clinical psychologist for one year."

To conduct psychological testing, one must have competence *in psychological testing*. This competence cannot merely be asserted, but must be shown to have developed through formal education, training, and experience (see Chapter Five). This point is relevant to the process of diagnosis, evaluation, or assessment more generally, even if testing were not involved. For example, when the diagnosis is based upon interview and observation, training and supervised experience in those assessment methods are necessary.

Understanding Measurement, Validation, and Research

Being able to document substantial course work, supervised training, and extensive experience in a given area of testing such as neuropsychological assessment of geriatric populations, intelligence testing of young children, or personality testing of adults helps a professional to establish competence in that area of testing in an ethics committee hearing, licensing hearing, or malpractice suit. But beyond this evidence of competence, one must also be able to demonstrate understanding of measurement, validation, and research.

Sanders and Keith-Spiegel (1980) described an APA ethics case in which a psychologist evaluated a person using a Minnesota Multiphasic Personality Inventory (MMPI), among other resources. The person who was evaluated felt that the test report, particularly the part based upon the MMPI results, was not accurate. All materials, including the test report and raw data, were eventually submitted to the APA Ethics Committee, which in turn submitted the materials for evaluation to two independent diplomates with expertise in testing.

The committee concluded that the psychologist did not demonstrate an adequate understanding of measurement, validation, and inference in his report: "The only test used by the complainee that has any established validity in identifying personality disorders is the MMPI, and none of the conclusions allegedly based on the MMPI are accurate. We suspect that the complainee's conclusions are based upon knowledge of a previous psychotic episode and information from the psychiatric consultant, whose conclusions seem to have been accepted uncritically. The complainee's report is a thoroughly unprofessional performance, in our opinion. Most graduate students would do much better" (Sanders & Keith-Spiegel, 1980, p. 1098).

Principle 2e of the "Ethical Principles of Psychologists" (APA, 1990a, p. 391) summarizes this requirement: "Psychologists responsible for decisions involving individuals or policies based on test results have an understanding of psychological or educational measurement, validation problems, and test research."

Ensuring That the Client Understands and Consents to Testing

Ensuring that a client fully understands the nature, purposes, and techniques of a given instrument helps to fulfill the client's right to give or withhold informed consent to any phase of assessment or treatment (see Chapter Seven). Determining that the client understands the testing is different from just providing information aloud or in written form. Some clients may be anxious, distracted, preoccupied, or so eager to please the clinician that they nod their heads as if to acknowledge that they understand an explanation when, in fact, they have understood none or little of the information. Some clients are unfamiliar with technical terms and concepts that the clinician tends to take for granted. Often this lack of communication is worsened by the clinician's eagerness to proceed with the testing and the client's fear of appearing ignorant.

It is the clinician's responsibility to make the necessary effort to provide a fully understandable explanation and to form a professional opinion regarding whether a client understands and consents. Principle 8a of the "Ethical Principles" (APA, 1990a, p. 394) defines this professional responsibility as follows: "In using assessment techniques, psychologists respect the right of clients to have full explanations of the nature and purpose of the techniques in language the client can understand, unless an explicit exception to this right has been agreed upon in advance. When the explanations are to be provided by others, psychologists establish procedures for ensuring the adequacy of these explanations."

Clarifying Access to the Test Report and Raw Data

Psychologists function within a complex framework of legal and ethical standards regarding the discretionary and mandatory release of test information. The Privacy Act of 1974, the California "truth in testing" statute, and *Detroit Edison v. National Labor Relations Board* are examples of federal and state legislation and case law that make test information more accessible to consumers.

The following fictional vignette illustrates the complex judgments psychologists may have to make regarding responsibilities to withhold or disclose assessment information:

A seventeen-year-old boy comes to your office and asks for a comprehensive psychological evaluation. He has been experiencing some headaches, anxiety, and depression. A high school dropout, he has been married for a year and has a one-year-old baby, but has left his wife and child and returned to live with his parents. He works full time as an auto mechanic and has insurance that covers the testing procedures.

You complete the testing. During the following year you receive requests for information about the testing from:

- the boy's physician, an internist
- the boy's parents, who are concerned about his depression
- the boy's employer, in connection with a worker's compensation claim filed by the boy
- the attorney for the insurance company that is contesting the worker's compensation claim
- the attorney for the boy's wife, who is suing for divorce and for custody of the baby
- the boy's attorney, who is considering suing you for malpractice because he does not like the results of the tests

Each of the requests asks for: the full formal report, the original test data, and copies of each of the tests you administered (for example, instructions and all items for the MMPI).

To which of these people are you ethically or legally obligated to supply all information requested, partial information, a summary of the report, or no information at all? For which requests is having the boy's written informed consent for release of information relevant?

There is no set of answers to these complex questions that would be generally applicable for all or even most readers. Each state has its own evolving legislation and case law that address, sometimes in an incomplete or confusing manner, clinician responsibilities. Such questions can, however, provide a basis for discussion in ethics courses, in clinical supervision and consultation, in staff meetings, or in workshops; answers can be sought that are relevant for a specific state. Practitioners may want to consider working through their state associations to develop clear guidelines to the current legal requirements. If the legal requirements in this or any other area of practice seem unethical, unreasonable, unclear, or potentially damaging to clients, practitioners may want to propose and support remedial legislation.

Following Standard Procedures
for Administering Tests

When we are reciting the instructions to the Wechsler Intelligence Scale for Children–Revised (WISC-R) or the Halstead Category Test for the five hundredth time, we may experience the urge to break the monotony, to get creative, to let our originality show through. And, particularly when we are in a hurry, we may want to abbreviate the instructions. After all, the client will catch on as the subtest progresses.

The assumption underlying standardized tests is that the test-taking situation and procedures are as similar as possible for everyone. When one departs from the procedures on which the norms are based, the standardized norms lose their direct applicability and the "standard" inferences drawn from those norms become questionable. Standard 6.2 of the *Standards for Educational and Psychological Testing* (APA, 1985, p. 41) states: "When a test user makes a substantial change in test format, mode of administration, instructions, language, or content, the user should revalidate the use of the test for the changed conditions or have a rationale supporting the claim that additional validation is not necessary or possible."

The Committee on Professional Standards of the APA (1984) published a finding that allowing a client to take home a test such as the MMPI departs from the "standard procedure." The "Casebook for providers of psychological services" (Committee on Professional Standards, 1984) describes a case in which a psychologist permitted his client to take home the MMPI to complete. When the complaint was filed with APA, the Committee on Professional Standards stated that whenever a psychologist "does not have direct, first-hand information as to the condition under which the test is taken, he or she is forced (in the above instance, unnecessarily) to assume that the test responses were not distorted by the general situation in which the test was taken (e.g., whether the client consulted others about test responses). Indeed the psychologist could have no assurance that this test was in fact completed by the client. In the instance where the test might be introduced as data in a court proceeding it would be summarily dismissed as hearsay evidence" (p. 664).

Awareness of Basic Assumptions

Our most fundamental asumptions or theoretical frameworks can significantly affect our assessments. Langer and Abelson's (1974) classic study, "A Patient by Any Other Name . . . ," for example, illustrates one way in which behavior therapists and psychoanalytically oriented therapists can differ when viewing the same individual: "Clinicians representing two different schools of thought, behavioral and analytic, viewed a single videotaped interview between a man who had recently applied for a new job and one of the authors. Half of each group was told that the interviewee was a 'job applicant,' while the remaining half was told that he was a 'patient.' At the end of the videotape, all clinicians were asked to complete a questionnaire evaluating the interviewee. The interviewee was described as fairly well adjusted by the behavioral therapists regardless of the label supplied. This was not the case, however, for the more traditional therapists. When the interviewee was labeled 'patient,' he was described as significantly more disturbed than he was when he was labeled 'job applicant'" (p. 4).

The point here is not whether either of these two orientations is more valid, reliable, respectable, empirically based, or useful, but rather to illustrate the obvious: Various basic theoretical orientations can lead to very different assessments. Psychologists conducting assessments and assigning diagnoses need to be continually aware of their own theoretical orientation and the ways in which this orientation is likely to affect the evaluation. Langer and Abelson (1974, p. 9) state clearly: "Despite the questionable light in which the analytic therapist group was cast in the present study, one strongly suspects that conditions might be arranged wherein the behavior therapists would fall into some kind of error, as much as the traditionalists. No single type of orientation toward clinical training is likely to avoid all types of biases or blind spots."

Awareness of Personal Factors
Leading to Misusing Diagnosis

In addition to a lack of awareness of our basic assumptions and our assumptions in specialty areas, insufficient attention to our own personal reactions and dynamics may tend to make us vulnerable to faulty evaluations. Reiser and Levenson's (1984) excellent article, "Abuses of the Borderline Diagnosis," focuses on six ways in which the diagnosis of borderline personality disorder is commonly abused "to express countertransference hate, mask imprecise thinking, excuse treatment failures, justify the therapist's acting out, defend against sexual clinical material, and avoid pharmacologic and medical treatment interventions" (p. 1528). Openness to such issues within ourselves and frequent consultations with colleagues can help prevent abuses of this kind and help ensure that our assessments meet the highest ethical standards.

Awareness of Financial Factors
Leading to Misusing Diagnosis

Third-party reimbursement has become so prevalent that most psychologists have become acutely aware of which diagnostic categories are "covered" and which are not. Unfortunately, the temptation to substitute a fraudulent but "covered" diagnosis for an honest but unreimbursable one can influence even senior and well-respected practitioners, as shown in a recent national study (Pope & Bajt, 1988). Kovacs (1987), in his strongly worded article on insurance billing, issues a stern warning that those "who are naive about insurance billing or who play a little fast and loose with carriers are beginning to play Russian Roulette. The carriers are now prepared to spend the necessary funds for investigators and for lawyers which will be required to sue in civil court and/or to bring criminal charges against colleagues who do not understand their ethical and legal responsibility in completing claim forms on behalf of their patients" (p. 24).

The article "Advice on Ethics of Billing Clients" (1987) in the *APA Monitor* lists among "billing practices that should be avoided": "Changing the diagnosis to fit reimbursement criteria"

(p. 42; see also Ethics Committee of the American Psychological Association, 1988).

Awareness of Gender Effects
and Cultural Influences

Sex-role stereotypes and other phenomena associated with gender and culture can influence the assessment process in diverse ways (see also Chapter Eleven). Three examples follow.

First, even tests thought to be "objective" and relatively free of bias can be vulnerable to such basic influences as the gender of the examiner. For example, some Wechsler Intelligence Scale for Children subtests not thought to involve gender bias were administered to schoolchildren (Pederson, Shinedling & Johnson, 1975). Both boys and girls achieved higher scores when the examiner was of the same gender as the test takers. This effect was especially pronounced for girls: They performed much better when the subtests were administered by a woman.

Second, Connie Hammen's work (personal communication, April 21, 1988; see also Golding, 1988) suggests that the frequently cited observation that many more women than men suffer from depression may be misleading. Part of the apparent difference may stem from a confusion of depressive mood or symptoms with the clinical syndrome of depression that meets specified diagnostic criteria. Another part of the apparent difference may be due to socialization: Women tend to be more open in acknowledging their depression. Still another part may be due to the specific set of symptoms sampled. For example, although young men and women tend to have comparable overall scores on comprehensive self-report assessments of depressive symptoms, women tend to check more items associated with self-criticism and emotional expressiveness while men tend to check more items associated with fatigue and physical complaints.

Third, Susan Cochran (personal communication, April 21, 1988) conducted a revealing study in which a self-description of a prospective female patient was distributed to a sample of therapists. Each therapist received the same self-description (which ran for about a page and a half), though half ended with the statement, "I believe my problem is depression," and the other half ended with the statement, "I believe my problem is sexual in nature." Each participant was asked to assess, on the basis of the self-description: (1) what is the nature of this individual's difficulty, (2) what would be the treatment of choice for a person who describes herself in these terms, and (3) would the therapist be willing to accept this referral? In addition to the closing statement indicating a self-diagnosis, Cochran introduced another experimental variable, involving the picture of the prospective patient at the top of the page: one-third of the therapists received a photo of a woman who was very attractive in conventional terms, one-third received a photo of a woman who was less attractive in conventional terms, and the remaining third received a photo of a woman who was still less attractive in conventional terms.

In responding to the first question — what was the diagnostic impression? — therapists who received pictures of a conventionally attractive woman tended to accept her self-diagnosis: If she said her problem was depression, they tended to accept that statement; if she said her problem was sexual in nature, they tended to agree. However, for women who were least conventionally attractive, if the patient indicated that her problem was sexual in nature, the therapist tended to agree but if she said that her problem was depression, the therapist tended to disagree and assert that it was probably sexual in nature.

In assessing the treatment of choice, therapists tended to think that the more conventionally attractive women would benefit from long-term individual psychotherapy while the less conventionally attractive women would benefit more from group therapy. In addition, the therapists in Cochran's study tended to invite referral of the women who were conventionally attractive and to suggest that the less conventionally attractive women be referred elsewhere.

Awareness of how such culture-related factors can distort the assessment process is crucial in eliminating or at least minimizing their pernicious effects.

Acknowledging the Low Base Rate Phenomenon

When a particular diagnostic category or an attribute being assessed rarely occurs in the population, ignoring this fact can lead to significant error in conducting evaluations. Even when the psychological tests are accurate, the statistical properties of a phenomenon with a low base rate can cause problems. Perhaps the most frequently cited example concerns assessing individuals for the potential for lethal violence: "Assume that one person out of a thousand will kill. Assume also that an exceptionally accurate test is created which differentiates with 95 percent effectiveness those who will kill from those who will not. If 100,000 people were tested, out of the 100 who would kill, 95 would be isolated. Unfortunately, out of the 99,900 who would not kill, 4,995 people would also be isolated as potential killers" (Livermore, Malmquist & Meehl, 1968, p. 84).

Awareness of Forensic Issues

Our society has become more litigious, and we tend to find ourselves, as psychologists, appearing in court more frequently or preparing documents that will become part of legal proceedings. Forensic settings set forth specific demands, and practitioners need to become aware of them. For example, financial factors (see previous section "Awareness of Financial Factors Leading to Misusing Diagnosis") can, under certain circumstances, create a bias—or at least the appearance of bias—in carrying out and reporting assessments. For this reason, forensic texts mandate that no psychologist accept a contingency fee. Blau (1984, p. 336) wrote: "The psychologist should never accept a fee contingent upon the outcome of a case." Shapiro (1990, p. 230) stated: "The expert witness should never, under any circumstances, accept a referral on a contingent fee basis." Only about 15 percent of the respondents in a recent national survey reported engaging in this practice (Pope, Tabachnick & Keith-Spiegel, 1987), and about the same percentage (14 percent) believe it to be good practice or good under most circumstances (Pope, Tabachnick & Keith-Spiegel, 1988).

Another potentially troublesome area in forensic practice involves conducting child custody assessments. Shapiro (1990, p. 99) for example, says that "under no circumstances should a report on child custody be rendered to the court, based on the evaluation of only one party to the conflict."

Frequent consultation with those who are well trained and experienced in forensic practice, particularly those who are Fellows of APA Division 41 and who hold a Forensic Diplomate, can be useful in becoming aware of and avoiding the pitfalls of conducting and reporting assessments in the forensic arena.

Attention to Potential Medical Causes

Particularly when a constellation of symptoms fits a well-known psychological diagnosis, it is tempting to ignore possible medical causes for a distress or disability (such as pain, weight loss, or bleeding from bodily orifices). A comprehensive evaluation, however, needs to rule out (or identify) possible medical causes. Rick Imbert, president of the American Professional Agency, stresses that "if there is any indication of a physical problem, then have a full medical screening; for example, symptoms which appear to be part of a schizophrenic process can actually be caused by a brain tumor" (personal communication, April 18, 1988).

Awareness of Prior Records of Assessment and Treatment

Prior records of assessment and treatment can be an invaluable resource as part of a comprehensive psychological evaluation. The courts have held that neglecting to make any effort to recognize, obtain, and use this resource violates, in some instances, the standard of care. In the federal case of *Jablonski v. United States* (1983), for example, the U.S. Ninth Circuit Court of Appeals upheld a "district court judge's findings of malpractice . . . for failure to obtain the past medical records."

Indicating All Reservations About Reliability and Validity

If any circumstances might have affected the results of psychological testing, such as dim lighting, frequent interruptions, a noisy environment, or medication, or if there is doubt that the person being tested shares all relevant characteristics with the reference groups on which the norms are based, these factors must be taken into account when interpreting test data and must be included in the formal report.

Principle 8c of the "Ethical Principles of Psychologists" (APA, 1990a) states, "In reporting assessment results, psychologists indicate any reservations that exist regarding validity or reliability because of the circumstances of the assessment or the inappropriateness of the norms for the person tested. Psychologists strive to ensure that the results of assessments and their interpretations are not misused by others" (P. 394).

Staying Current

Finally, it is important to remain abreast of the current literature, of the innovations and evolving state of the art and science in the area of diagnosis, testing, and assessment. Irving Weiner (1989), editor of the *Journal of Personality Assessment,* discussed the extremely rapid accumulation of new data relevant to virtually all forms of psychological testing. To fall behind, according to Weiner, is to practice incompetently and thus unethically: "The passage of just a few years . . . is sufficient to land practitioners who have not kept current on the doorstep of unethicality" (p. 830).

9

Sexual Relationships
with Clients

One of the oldest ethical mandates in the health care professions is the prohibition against engaging in sexual intimacies with a patient. Brodsky (1989) notes that this rule is in fact older than the 2,500-year-old Hippocratic Oath; it was mentioned in the even more ancient code of the Nigerian healing arts. That this prohibition has remained constant over so long a time and throughout so many diverse cultures reflects to some extent the recognition that such intimacies place the patient at risk for exceptional harm.

Until relatively recently, our understanding of therapist-client sexual involvement was based mainly upon theory, common sense, and individual case studies. Only in the past twenty years has a considerable body of diverse systematic investigations informed our understanding with empirical data. Some of the findings will be summarized in this chapter. (For more detailed presentations of this research, see Gabbard, 1989, and Pope, 1990b & 1990c.)

Injured Clients

Beginning with Masters and Johnson (1966, 1970, 1975), a number of investigators have examined how therapist-client sexual involvement affects clients (Bouhoutsos, Holroyd, Lerman, Forer & Greenberg, 1983; Brown, 1988; Butler & Zelen, 1977; Feldman-Summers & G. Jones, 1984; Herman, Gartrell, Olarte, Feldstein & Localio, 1987; Sonne, Meyer, Borys & Marshall, 1985; Vinson, 1987). Approaches to learning about effects have included studies of clients who have returned to therapy with a subsequent therapist as well as those who undertook no further therapy after their sexual involvement with a therapist. The consequences for clients who have been sexually involved with a psychotherapist have been compared to those for matched groups of therapy clients who have not been sexually involved with a therapist and of patients who have been sexually involved with a (nontherapist) physician. Subsequent treating therapists (of those clients who undertook a subsequent therapy), independent clinicians, and the clients themselves have evaluated the effects. Standardized psychological assessment instruments have supplemented clinical interview and behavioral observation. These diverse approaches to systematic study have supplemented individual patients' firsthand accounts (Bates & Brodsky, 1989; Freeman & Roy, 1976; Plaisil, 1985; Walker & Young, 1986).

The consequences for the clients seem to cluster into ten very general categories: (1) ambivalence, (2) guilt, (3) emptiness and isolation, (4) sexual confusion, (5) impaired ability to trust, (6) confused roles and boundaries, (7) emotional liability, (8) suppressed rage, (9) increased suicidal risk, and (10) cognitive dysfunction, frequently in the areas of concentration and memory and often involving flashbacks, intrusive thoughts, unbidden images, and nightmares (Pope, 1988b).

Perpetrators

How many therapists engage in sexual intimacies with their clients? Estimates are generally based upon anonymous surveys. The six national surveys that have been published in peer-reviewed journals suggest a fairly consistent decrease in the rate of such involvement from 12.0–12.1 percent for male therapists and 2.6–3.0 percent for female therapists in the earliest two surveys to 0.9–3.6 percent for male therapists and 0.2–0.5 percent in the two most recent surveys (Borys & Pope, 1989; Gartrell, Herman, Olarte, Feldstein & Localio, 1986; Holroyd & Brodsky, 1977; Pope, Keith-Spiegel & Tabachnick, 1986; Pope, Levenson & Schover, 1979; Pope, Tabachnick & Keith-Spiegel, 1987). It is possible that this decrease is genuine and has resulted from such factors as the increasing criminalization of this behavior, the decreasing tendency for professionals to remain silent about the scope and nature of abuse, and the increased awareness among patients about how to file complaints. The decline may also represent increasingly less candid reporting (due, for example, to the growing number of states in which therapist-patient sexual intimacy has become a felony) than to changes in actual behavior.

The only study surveying psychiatrists, psychologists, and social workers sent the same form to all 4,800 clinicians included in the sample and found no significant differences among the professions in the self-reported rates at which they engaged in sex with clients (Borys & Pope, 1989).

The surveys do reveal a consistent trend: Male therapists engage in sex with their clients at much higher rates than female therapists do. Holroyd and Brodsky (1977), for example, found that 85 percent of the self-reported incidents of therapist-patient sex involved male therapists.

Bates and Brodsky (1989) examined the various risk factors that have been hypothesized, at one time or another, to make certain clients more vulnerable to sexual exploitation by a therapist. Their analysis led them not to the personal history or characteristics of the client but rather to prior behavior of the therapist: The most effective predictor of whether a client will become sexually involved with a therapist is whether that therapist has previously engaged in sex with a client (Bates & Brodsky, 1989). With access to a considerable set of historical and actuarial data, the APA Insurance Trust (1990, p. 3) revealed that "the recidivism rate for sexual misconduct is substantial." Holroyd and Brodsky's (1977) landmark survey found that 80 percent of the therapists who reported engaging in therapist-patient sexual intimacies indicated that they became involved with more than one patient. More recently, the California

Department of Consumer Affairs (1990) published its findings in a document that was sent to all licensed therapists and counselors in California and that must, according to California law, be provided by a therapist to any patient who reports having been sexually involved with a prior therapist. This document notes that "80 percent of the sexually exploiting therapists have exploited more than one client. In other words, if a therapist is sexually exploiting a client, chances are he or she has done so before" (p. 14).

Not all perpetrators limit their sexual involvement to adult patients. A national survey found a significant number of cases of therapist-client sexual intimacies involving minor children (Bajt & Pope, 1989). The average age of the boys was twelve years and six months, with a range from sixteen down to seven. The average age of the girls was thirteen years and nine months, with a range of seventeen down to three years old.

Beyond the Prohibition

The issue of therapist-client sexual intimacies focuses many of the major themes of this book. The great vulnerability of the client highlights the power of the therapist and the trust that must characterize the client's relationship with the therapist. The therapist's caring may be crucial in protecting against the temptation to exploit the client.

The issue of therapist-client sexual intimacy also illustrates ethics as more than the following of a list of "do's and don't's," as discussed in Chapter Four. There is, of course, a clear prohibition: Avoid any sexual intimacies with clients. No cause, situation, or condition could ever legitimize such intimacies with any client (see, for example, Gabbard & Pope, 1989). The prohibition stands as a fundamental ethical mandate no matter what the rationalizations. Taking this prohibition seriously and adhering to it without exception, however, mark the initial rather than the final steps in meeting our ethical responsibilities in this area. Several associated issues that we must confront and struggle with follow.

Physical Contact with Clients

The very topic of therapist-client sexual involvement as well as concern that we may be subject to an ethics complaint or malpractice suit may make many of us very nervous. We may go to great lengths to ensure that we maintain physical distance from our clients and under no circumstances touch them for fear that this might be misconstrued. A similar phenomenon seems to be occurring in regard to increasing public acknowledgment of child sexual abuse: Adults may be reluctant to hold children and to engage in nonsexual touch that is a normal part of life.

Is there any evidence that nonsexual touching of patients is actually associated with therapist-client sexual intimacy? Holroyd and Brodsky (1980) examined this question and found no indications that physical contact with patients made sexual contact more likely. They *did* find evidence that differential touching of male and female clients (that is, touching clients of one gender significantly more than clients of the other gender) was associated with sexual intimacies: "Erotic contact not leading to intercourse is associated with older, more experienced therapists who do not otherwise typically touch their patients at a rate different from other therapists (except when mutually initiated). Sexual intercourse with patients is associated with the touching of opposite-sex patients but not same-sex patients. It is the differential application of touching — rather than touching per se — that is related to intercourse" (p. 810).

If the therapist is personally comfortable engaging in physical contact with a patient, maintains a theoretical orientation for which therapist-client contact is not antithetical, and has competence (education, training, and supervised experience) in the use of touch, then the decision of whether or not to make physical contact with a particular client must be based on a careful evaluation of the clinical needs of the client at that moment. When solidly based upon clinical needs and a clinical rationale, touch can be exceptionally caring, comforting, reassuring, or healing. When not justified by clinical need and therapeutic rationale, nonsexual touch can also be experienced as intrusive, frightening, or demeaning. The decision must always be made carefully and in full awareness of the power of the therapist and the trust (and vulnerability) of the client.

Our responsibility to be sensitive to the issues of nonsexual touch and to explore them carefully extends to other therapeutic issues conceptually related to the issue of therapist-client sexual involvement. Our unresolved concerns with therapist-client sexual intimacies may prompt us to respond to the prospect of nonsexual touching either phobically — avoiding in an exaggerated manner any contact or even physical closeness with a client — or counterphobically — engaging in apparently nonsexual touching such as handshakes and hugs as if to demonstrate that we are very comfortable with physical intimacy and experience no sexual impulses. These unresolved concerns can also elicit phobic or counterphobic behavior in other areas, such as the clinician's initiating or focusing on sexual issues to an extent that is not based on the client's clinical needs. To respond ethically, authentically, and therapeutically to such issues, we must come to terms with our own unresolved feelings of sexual attraction to our clients.

Sexual Attraction to Clients

Sexual attraction to clients is a common occurrence. A national survey of psychologists provided information about this phenomenon (Pope, Keith-Spiegel & Tabachnick, 1987). A vast majority (87 percent) of the counselors and therapists reported that they had experienced attraction toward a client. Attraction was experienced by a greater percentage of male (95 percent) than of female (76 percent) clinicians.

The overwhelming majority (82 percent) of clinicians who reported experiencing attraction noted that they never seriously considered engaging in sex with the client. Nevertheless, merely experiencing the attraction made most (63 percent) of the therapists feel "guilty, anxious, or confused" (p. 147). One-fifth of them kept the attraction a complete secret; they did not mention it to the client, to their supervisor, or to their own therapist. Over one-fourth of them reported having sexual fantasies about a client while engaging in sex with someone else.

The topic of sexual attraction to clients was absent from the graduate school and internship training of many of the therapists in this national survey. Only 9 percent believed that their training in this area was adequate. It is an ethical responsibility of those who teach and supervise therapists to provide adequate training in these issues and to ensure that the training setting or supervisory relationship is a safe and supportive environment for learning (see Chapter Fourteen).

For any of us who experience sexual attraction to a client, it is important to recognize that the research suggests that this is a common experience. To feel attraction to a client is *not* unethical; to acknowledge and address the attraction promptly, carefully, and adequately is an important ethical responsibility. For some of us, consultation with respected colleagues will be useful. For others, obtaining formal supervision for our work with that client may be necessary. For still others, entering or reentering psychotherapy can be helpful.

Responding to Victimized Patients

It is not unlikely that any therapist, counselor, or trainee reading this book will encounter clients who have been sexually victimized by a prior therapist. A national study of 1,320 psychologists found that 50 percent reported working with at least one client who, in the therapist's professional opinion, had been a victim of therapist-client sexual intimacies (Pope & Vetter, in press). Only 4 percent reported working with at least one client who, in the therapist's opinion, had made false allegations about sex with a prior therapist.

It is crucial that clinicians working with such clients be genuinely knowledgeable about this area (see Chapter Five). Clients who have been sexually exploited tend to be exceptionally vulnerable to revictimization when their clinical needs are not recognized. Special methods and considerations for providing therapeutic services to victims of therapist-patient sexual intimacies have been developed and continue to evolve (see, for example, Pope & Bouhoutsos, 1986; Sonne, 1989; Sonne, Meyer, Borys & Marshall, 1985; Sonne & Pope, in press).

Ethical Aspects of Rehabilitation

Unfortunately, therapists and counselors may act in ways that discount the harm done by perpetrators of therapist-patient sex, that obscure the responsibilities of perpetrators, and that enable perpetrators to continue—sometimes after a period of suspension—victimizing clients (Bates & Brodsky, 1989; Gabbard, 1989). The rehabilitation methods by which perpetrators are returned to practice focus many of this book's themes and pose difficult ethical dilemmas. Pope (1990c) reviewed some of the crucial but difficult ethical questions facing therapists and counselors considering rehabilitation efforts; they are summarized below.

     Competence. Does the clinician who is implementing the rehabilitation plan possess demonstrable competence (see Chapter Five) in the areas of rehabilitation and of therapist-patient sexual intimacies?

     Has the rehabilitation method the clinician uses been adequately validated through independent studies? (See the section "Approaches, Strategies, and Techniques" in Chapter Five.) Obviously, if the clinician were claiming an effective "cure" for pedophilia, kleptomania, dyslexia, panic attacks, or a related disorder, that clinician would need to present the scientific evidence for the intervention's effectiveness. Ethical standards for claims *based on evidence* in this area—particularly given the risks for abuse to which future patients may be exposed—should not be waived. Such evidence must meet the customary requirement of publication in peer-reviewed scientific or professional journals. As Pope (1990c, p. 482) noted, "Research results that survive and benefit from this painstaking process of systematic review created to help ensure the scientific integrity, merit, and trustworthiness of new findings may be less likely (than data communicated *solely* through press conferences, popular lectures, books, workshops, and television appearances) to contribute to what Tavris (1987) terms 'social-science fiction.' " We have been unable to locate any independently conducted, replicated research published in peer-reviewed scientific or professional journals that supports the effectiveness of rehabilitation efforts in this area.

Informed Consent. Whether the rehabilitation technique is viewed as an intervention of proven effectiveness (through independently conducted research trials) or an experimental research trial for a promising approach, have those who are put at risk for harm been adequately informed and been given the option of not assuming the risk, should the rehabilitation fail to be 100 percent effective? (See the section "Failing to Provide Informed Consent" in Chapter Seven.)

Assessment. Do the research trials investigating the potential effectiveness of the rehabilitation method meet at least minimal professional standards (see Chapter Eight)? For example, is the research conducted independently? (We are rarely disinterested judges of the profundity, effectiveness, and near-perfection of our own work.)

A more complex requirement concerns whether the base rate of discovery of abuse is adequately taken into account in conducting and reporting the results of experimental trials of rehabilitation efforts. Perpetrators may continue to engage in sexual intimacies with clients during (or after) rehabilitation efforts, even when they are supervised (see, for example, Bates & Brodsky, 1989). The abuse may only come to light if the client reports it. Yet the base rate of such reports by clients is quite low. Surveys of victims suggest that only about 5 percent report the behavior to a licensing board. The percentage appears to be significantly lower when the number of instances of abuse estimated from anonymous surveys of clinicians (who report instances in which they have engaged in abuse) are compared with complaints filed with licensing boards, ethics committees, and the civil and criminal courts. Using the higher 5 percent reporting estimate, assume that you conduct research in which a licensing board refers ten offenders to you for rehabilitation. You work with the offenders for several years and are convinced that you have completely rehabilitated all ten. You assure the licensing board of your complete confidence that none of the ten will pose any risk to future clients. But also assume that your rehabilitation effort fails miserably: All ten offenders will engage in sex with a future client. What are the probabilities that *any* of the ten future abuse victims will file a complaint? If each client has only a 5 percent probability of reporting the abuse, there is a 59.9 percent probability that *none* of the ten will file a complaint. Thus there is close to a 60 percent chance that these research trials, even if independently evaluated, will appear to validate your approach as 100 percent effective, when in fact it was 100 percent ineffective. If ignored in conducting and reporting research, the low base rate can make a worthless intervention appear completely reliable.

Power and Trust. The ethics of psychotherapy and counseling are inherently related to power and trust (see Chapter Three). How are these factors relevant to the dilemmas of rehabilitation?

If a judge were convicted of abusing the power and trust inherent in the position of judgeship by allowing bribes to determine the outcome of cases, numerous sanctions, both criminal and civil, might follow. However, even after the judge "paid the debt" due society by the abuse of power and trust, the judge would not be allowed to resume the bench, regardless of any "rehabilitation."

Similarly, if a preschool director were discovered to have sexually abused the students, he or she would likely face both civil and criminal penalties. The director might undergo extensive rehabilitation efforts to help reduce the risk that he or she would engage in further abuse of children. However, regardless of the effectiveness of the rehabilitation efforts, the state would not issue the individual a new license to found and direct another preschool.

Neither of these two offenders would necessarily be precluded from practicing their professions. The former judge and preschool director, once rehabilitated, might conduct research, consult, publish, lecture, or pursue other careers within the legal and educational fields. However, serving as judge or as preschool director are positions that involve such trust — by both society and the individuals subject to their immediate power — that the violation of such an important and clearly understood prohibition against abuse of trust (and power) precludes the opportunity to hold such special positions within the fields of law and education.

The helping professions must consider the ethical, practical, and policy implications of allowing and enabling offenders to resume the positions of special trust that they abused. Do psychotherapy and counseling involve or require a comparable degree of inviolable trust, from individual clients and from the society more generally, and ethical integrity as the positions of judge and preschool director within the legal and educational fields?

Therapists violate their patients' trust not only when they enter into sexual relationships with patients but also when they establish other distinct additional relationships that place the patient at risk for harm. Chapter Ten focuses on these nonsexual dual relationships.

10

Nonsexual
Dual Relationships

Dual relationships are relatively easy to define; they are much more difficult for many of us to recognize in our practice. A dual relationship in psychotherapy occurs when the therapist is in another, significantly different relationship with one of his or her patients. Most commonly, the second role is social, financial, or professional.

In some cases, one relationship follows the other. The mere fact that the two roles are apparently sequential rather than clearly concurrent does not, in and of itself, mean that the two relationships do not constitute a dual relationship. Most of the important relationships in our lives have at least some sort of carry over. Thus a therapist would avoid treating her ex-husband although they were divorced and the marriage was clearly over.

In part it may be the relative simplicity and abstraction of the definition that lulls many of us into ignoring the diverse ways, many of them exceptionally subtle, that dual relationships occur in psychotherapy, often with potentially devastating results. Specific examples, more than abstract definitions, may provide us with a useful awareness of how these entanglements occur. The following three fictional scenarios, dismayingly typical of actual practice, illustrate nonsexual dual relationships. (As mentioned previously, the vignettes are not based on actual cases or individuals.)

Fictional Vignette 1

Rosa, an attorney, is going through one of the worst times in her life. For several weeks, she had been experiencing mild abdominal discomfort and had dismissed it as a muscle strained while jogging or nervousness about the case she was preparing to argue in her first appearance before the state supreme court. The pains become worse and she manages to drive herself to the emergency room. A rather brusk medical resident informs her that he has located a large lump on her ovary. He advises her to make an appointment to undergo extensive tests to determine the nature of the lump, which may be cancerous. Rosa is terrified. The tests are scheduled for two days from now. She has to cope not only with the pain but also with the uncertainty of what the physicians will discover. She goes immediately to the house of her best friend, June, a psychotherapist. June suggests showing Rosa some self-hypnotic and imagery techniques that might help her cope with her pain and anxiety. As June leads her through the exercises, Rosa begins to feel relieved and comforted. However, when she tries to use the techniques by herself, she experiences no effects at all. June agrees to lead her through the hypnotic and imagery exercises two or three times a day until the medical crisis is resolved. During the fourth meeting, spontaneous images that are quite troubling begin occurring. Rosa starts talking about them and feels they are related to things that happened to her as a little child. She discusses them in detail with June, and by the end of the sixth session, June recognizes that an intense transference has developed. She encourages Rosa to consult another therapist but Rosa refuses, saying that there is no one else she could trust with these matters and that terminating the sessions would make her feel so betrayed and abandoned that she fears she would take her own life.

Fictional Vignette 2

Bill has just opened a private practice office and has exactly two patients. One of them, Mr. Lightfoot, is an

extremely successful investment analyst who is grateful to
Bill for all the benefits Mr. Lightfoot is getting from psychotherapy. The worst of Mr. Lightfoot's depression seems
to be in remission and he is now focusing on his relationships to those whose financial matters he handles. Bill, who
genuinely likes Mr. Lightfoot, finds himself especially attentive when his patient talks about new investment opportunities. Unexpectedly, Mr. Lightfoot says that Bill
might make a great deal of money if he invests in a certain
project that is now being planned. The more Bill thinks
about it, the more this seems like a terrific opportunity.
It will help Mr. Lightfoot's sense of self-esteem because he
will be in the position of helping Bill rather than always
receiving help from him. It will not cost Mr. Lightfoot anything. Finally, it may allow Bill to survive in private practice and thus enable him to continue to help others. (Bill's
overhead was greater than expected, the anticipated referrals were just not materializing, and he was down to his
last $10,000 in savings, which would not last long given
his office rent and other expenses.) He decides to give his
savings to Mr. Lightfoot to invest for him.

Fictional Vignette 3

Dr. Ali is a successful psychotherapist who now owns
and manages his own mental health clinic. Lately, he has
noticed that his normally outstanding secretary, Mr. Miller,
has been making numerous mistakes, some of them resulting in considerable financial losses for the clinic. Dr. Ali's
customary toleration, encouragement, and nonjudgmental
pointing out of the errors have not improved his secretary's
performance. He decides that a serious and frank discussion of the situation is necessary. When he begins talking
with his secretary about the deteriorating performance, Mr.
Miller begins telling him about some personal and financial stresses that he has been encountering that make it
difficult for him to attend to his work. Dr. Ali is aware that
his secretary cannot afford therapy and that the chances
of hiring a new secretary with anywhere near Mr. Miller's

previous level of skills is at best a long shot. Even if a good secretary could be found in what is a cutthroat job market, there would be a long period of orientation and training during which Dr. Ali anticipates he would continue to lose revenue. He decides that the only course of action that makes sense, that creatively solves all problems, is for Dr. Ali to take on Mr. Miller as a patient for two or three hours each week until Mr. Miller has a chance to work through his problems. Mr. Miller could continue to work as secretary and would not be charged for the therapy sessions. Dr. Ali would provide them without charge as part of a creative and generous "employee benefit."

Problems with Dual Relationships

As these fictional scenarios illustrate and as the clinical and research literature have discussed, dual relationships jeopardize professional judgment, clients' welfare, and the process of therapy itself (see, for example, Borys & Pope, 1989; Ethics Committee of the American Psychological Association, 1988b; Keith-Spiegel & Koocher, 1985; Pope, 1988a). Some of the major difficulties with dual relationships follow.

First, the dual relationship erodes and distorts the professional nature of the therapeutic relationship, which is secured within a reliable set of boundaries upon which both therapist and patient can depend. When the therapist is also the patient's lover, landlord, best friend, or employer, the crucial professional nature of the therapeutic relationship is compromised. Note that terming the therapeutic relationship "professional" in no way implies that it is or needs to be cold, distant, unfeeling, uncaring, or otherwise stereotypical of the worst professionals.

Second, dual relationships create conflicts of interest and thus compromise the disinterest (*not* lack of interest) necessary for sound professional judgment. The therapist as professional professes to place the interests of the patient foremost (except in those rare instances in which to do so would place third parties at unacceptable risk for harm). But if the therapist allows another relationship to occur, the therapist creates a second set of interests to which he or she will be subject. Thus the therapist who is treating a friend may be reluctant to allow the patient to explore options that may upset the therapist's social network; additionally, the patient may be afraid to explore such options. The therapist who is treating a patient in exchange for some services may find himself or herself manipulating or otherwise influencing the patient to provide better services or might become so critical of the patient's seemingly poor services that the therapeutic process becomes destructive for the patient. In dual relationships, the therapist is engaged in meeting his or her own needs (for example, sexual or social). Further, in dual relationship therapies, recognition, analysis, and management of transference and countertransference become all but impossible.

Third, dual relationships would affect the cognitive processes that research has shown to play a role in the beneficial effects of therapy and which help the patient to maintain the benefits of therapy after termination (see Gabbard & Pope, 1989).

Fourth, because of the therapist-patient relationship, the patient cannot enter into a business or other secondary relationship with the therapist on equal footing (see Pope, 1988a). One aspect of the power differential is as follows. When we believe we have been wronged by, say, our plumber or nextdoor neighbor, we can attempt various methods to resolve the difficulty and, if those methods are unsuccessful, we can take the matter to court. But the patient who feels seriously wronged in a business, financial, or social transaction with his or her therapist faces troubling obstacles in seeking legal redress. The therapist can use the "secrets" and intensely private material about the patient that the therapist became aware of during the psychotherapy in planning the most effective defense. Further, therapists may use a variety of false diagnostic labels by which to discredit the patient, a practice that is unfortunately common (Pope, 1988a).

Fifth, if it became acceptable practice for therapists to engage in dual financial, social, and professional relationships with their patients, whether prior or subsequent to termination, then the nature of psychotherapy would be drastically changed. Psychotherapists could begin using their practices to screen their patients for each patient's likelihood of meeting—either during therapy or some time after termination—the therapists' social, sexual, financial, or professional needs or desires. The lonely therapist could look for patients whom he or she might like to socialize with after termination. The therapist who wanted a second (or subsequent) career in the film industry could keep an eye out for a famous but troubled screenwriter with whom the therapist could collaborate on scripts, either as part of the process of therapy or after waiting a suitable time after termination. Therapists could use their practices as a dating service, looking for prospective dates or mates (the therapist being in an exceptionally good position to learn about the prospect before actually asking them out after termination). If dual relationships were acceptable, patients also would learn that therapists were available for extratherapeutic possibilities (perhaps after termination) and could alter their behavior accordingly.

Sixth, both during the course of therapy and at any time after, the therapist may be invited or compelled (through subpoena or court order) to offer testimony regarding the patient's diagnosis, treatment, or prognosis. Such testimony may be crucial to the patient in personal injury suits, custody hearings, criminal trials, and other judicial proceedings. If the therapist was also the business partner, live-in lover, or "we frequently share vacations together" type of friend, the objectivity, reliability, and integrity of the testimony as well as the information and documents reflecting the therapy (such as chart notes and insurance form diagnoses) become suspect.

Explicit Standards and Mechanisms of Accountability

Dual relationships form the major basis of licensing disciplinary actions, of financial losses in malpractice suits involving psychologists, and of ethics complaints against psychologists (see Chapter Two). Vested with statutory authority to protect consumers from harm or abuse by therapists, licensing boards originally addressed dual relationships by focusing mainly on allegations of sexual dual relationships (for example, *Colorado State Board of Medical Examiners v. Weiler,* 1965; *Cooper v. Board of Medical Examiners,* 1975; *Morra v. State Board of Examiners of Psychologists,* 1973; see also Chapter Nine). In the past decade, however, state licensing boards have addressed more vigorously — in words and actions — the issue of nonsexual dual relationships, particularly bartering of professional services. For example, the California licensing boards distributed to all licensed therapists in the state a pamphlet emphasizing that "hiring a client to do work for the therapist, or bartering goods or services to pay for therapy" constituted "inappropriate behavior and misuse of power" (California Department of Consumer Affairs, 1990, p. 3). This statement reflects the formal policy interpretation that the APA Ethics Committee approved during its February 1982 meeting that "bartering of personal services is a violation of Principle 6a" (see also Ethics Committee of the APA, 1988b; Keith-Spiegel & Koocher, 1985). Similarly, some licensing boards have imposed periods of suspension and additional terms following investigations of allegations concerning nonsexual dual relationships. Licensing boards' attention to such cases may parallel the APA's highlighting of nonsexual dual relationship ethics cases (1987a, pp. 79–85), the formal resolutions of which were intended by the association (p. vii) to serve as precedents for national, state, and local ethics committees of psychologists (see also Ethics Committee of the APA, 1988b; Keith-Spiegel & Koocher, 1985).

A Review of Recent Research

There has been considerable research regarding sexual dual relationships (see Chapter Nine). Research concerning the prevalence of nonsexual dual relationships, however, has been relatively rare.

Tallman (1981; cited in Keith-Spiegel & Koocher, 1985) conducted perhaps the earliest study on nonsexual dual relationships. Of the thirty-eight psychotherapists participating, about 33 percent indicated that they had formed social relationships with at least some of their patients. An intriguing aspect of the findings was that, although only half of the participants were male, *all* of the therapists who developed these social relationships with patients were male. This significant gender difference is remarkably consistent not only in terms of both sexual and nonsexual dual relationships in psychotherapy but also in terms of dual relationships involving teaching and supervision. Borys and Pope (1989, p. 290) summarize the research that has accumulated over the past dozen or so years: "First, the significant difference (i.e., a greater proportion of male than of female psychologists) that characterizes sexualized dual relationships conducted by both therapists and educators (teachers, clinical supervisors, and administrators) also characterizes nonsexual dual relationships conducted by therapists in the areas of social/financial involvements and dual professional roles. Male respondents tended to rate social/financial involvements and dual professional roles as more ethical and reported engaging in these involvements with more clients than did female respondents. Second, the data suggest that male therapists tend to engage in nonsexual dual relationships more with female clients than with male clients. . . . Third, these trends hold for psychologists, psychiatrists, and clinical social workers." Note that these statistical analyses take into account the fact that most therapists are male and most patients are female.

Pope, Tabachnick, and Keith-Spiegel (1987) included several items regarding nonsexual dual relationships — "accepting services from a client in lieu of fee," "providing therapy to one of your friends," "going into business with a former client" — in their survey of the ethical beliefs and practices of 1,000 clinical psychologists (return rate = 46 percent). Their findings were consistent with a larger scale multidisciplinary study focusing on dual relationships reported in the next paragraph.

A survey of 1,600 psychiatrists, 1,600 psychologists, and 1,600 social workers (with a 49 percent return rate) examined beliefs and behaviors regarding a range of dual relationships in the light of such factors as therapist gender, profession (psychiatrist, psychologist, social worker), therapist age, experience, marital status, region of residence, client gender, practice setting (such as solo or group private practice and outpatient clinics), practice locale (size of the community), and theoretical orientation (Borys & Pope, 1989). The survey's findings included these three points:

1. There was no significant difference among the professions in terms of sexual intimacies with clients before or after termination (see Chapter Nine) or in terms of nonsexual dual professional roles, social involvements, or financial involvements with patients.
2. The percentage of therapists who rated each dual relationship behavior as ethical under most or all conditions was invariably less than the percentage of therapists viewing it as never ethical or ethical under only some or rare conditions.
3. Although psychologists alone explicitly prohibit nonsexual dual relationships in their ethical standards (APA, 1990a), psychiatrists tend, as a whole, to view such relationships as less ethical than do psychologists or social workers.

In a separate analysis of these data, Borys (1988, p. 181) found that "there was a clear relationship between sexual and nonsexual dual role behaviors" (see also Ethics Committee of the American Psychological Association, 1988b). She used a systems perspective to explore this association between nonsexual and sexual dual relationships: "As with familial incest, sexual involvement between therapist and client may be the culmination of a more general breakdown in roles and relationship boundaries which begin on a nonsexual level. This link was predicted by the systems perspective, which views disparate roles and behaviors within a relational system as interrelated. Changes in one arena are expected to affect those in other realms of behavior. The results of the current study suggest that the role boundaries and norms in the therapeutic relationship, just as those in the family, serve a protective function that serves to prevent exploitation" (p. 182).

These studies of nonsexual dual relationships in psychotherapy provide some initial empirical data upon which to develop an understanding of the phenomenon and provide some intriguing hypotheses. What is striking, however, is the scarcity of such studies. We need critical self-study, including the systematic collection of data, regarding the occurrence and effects of dual relationships.

Strategies of Toleration and Justification

If both sexual and nonsexual dual relationships have historically been viewed by the mental health professions as harmful, what strategies enable us to tolerate or justify them? Any answer, at least at this stage, can only be speculative, but such speculation may help generate research hypotheses and prompt more thoughtful consideration of any temptations we may feel to engage in harmful dual relationships with our patients. Perhaps part of the answer lies in the consistent research finding that for not only sexual but also nonsexual dual relationships in therapy (as well as for dual relationships in teaching, supervision, and administration), the perpetrators are overwhelmingly (but not exclusively) male and the victims are overwhelmingly (but not exclusively) female. Reflecting the larger society, the mental health professions unfortunately seem exceptionally resourceful in finding ways to deny, justify, trivialize, and discount forms of serious harm for which the perpetrators are mostly men and the victims are mostly women (Pope, 1990b; Walker & Young, 1986). Perhaps another part of the answer lies in some of the strategies outlined below.

Selective Inattention. One of the most prevalent ways in which dual relationships — and many other forms of unethical behavior — are made tolerable is through selective inattention. The therapist blocks out sustained, useful awareness of the duality of relationships by splitting the two relationships and refusing to acknowledge that both relationships involve the same patient and have implications for the patient and the patient's treatment.

Selective inattention is a more advanced version of carelessness or negligence, and all of us who have maintained a clinical practice have likely engaged in it in one form or another.

For example, we may have been treating a patient and have found ourselves becoming terribly drowsy or bored during a session. Such feelings may have important implications for the treatment of that patient and may represent an evolving countertransference reaction. However, attending to such feelings may make us uncomfortable and we may choose to treat them carelessly, trying to ease or shove them out of our awareness and to split off any remaining awareness we have of those feelings from our considerations about this particular patient and the treatment. As another example, we may work in a hospital and find ourselves talking with other treatment and clerical staff about patients over lunch in the hospital cafeteria. At the end of the day, were anyone to ask us, we would deny having breached any patient's confidentiality, having blocked off awareness that chatting about patients in an informal public setting, such as a hospital cafeteria, violates our responsibilities to safeguard the privacy of our patients and their treatment.

One indication that selective inattention may have played a role in the development of a dual relationship is the lack of any mention of a second relationship in the treatment notes. Thus anyone reviewing the patient's chart would be completely unaware that the therapist has formed a business partnership with the patient, has borrowed next month's rent from the patient, or has moved into the same house with the patient. The chart contains no mention of the duality of the relationship, no consideration of how the two relationships may be interacting, and no discussion of how the dual relationship may affect the patient's clinical status, prognosis, treatment plan, or response to the treatment plan. The form for informed consent to treatment will also lack any information regarding how the dual relationship may affect the treatment.

Selective inattention may foster dual relationships in another manner. Often the colleagues of a therapist who is entering a dual relationship may choose to screen out and remain selectively inattentive to evidence that the therapist is engaging in activities that put the patient at risk for harm. Again, such selective inattention regarding some of our closest colleagues is common to virtually all of us who practice as clinicians. At times, we may not want to risk losing a friendship; we fear that the warmth of our relationship with a colleague who is engaging in a harmful dual relationship with a patient might disappear, perhaps permanently. At times, we may fear the anger or the power of our colleague. Perhaps she is our employer or supervisor; perhaps he is a valuable source of referrals. At times, we may not want to rock the boat and upset the tranquility of a formal organization, such as a clinic, or an informal network of colleagues. And at times, we may experience the "glass house" phenomenon: We may avoid raising ethical issues with others because we are afraid that they will begin raising them with us. Thus we may enter into a tacit pact with our colleagues: Everyone will ignore everyone else's ethical violations. In such situations, selective inattention becomes an important aspect of the interpersonal or social ecology. When selective inattention becomes the norm, any attempt to overcome the splitting off of awareness must overcome the tendency of the interpersonal or social system to maintain homeostasis. The accumulated resistance to acknowledging the duality of the treatment relationship becomes quite powerful.

Benefits. A second way in which dual relationships are sometimes justified is that they are beneficial for the patient. When the initial malpractice suits alleging sexual dual relationships were tried, defendants frequently stressed that the sexual relationship was an important component of the treatment plan. The addition of the sexual relationship was said to provide the patient with a more nurturing, less coldly professional relationship; a more complete sense of acceptance; a way for the patient to experience and work through "overt transference"; and a safe "bridge" between the therapeutic and nontherapeutic environment (that is, the patient could "try out" on the therapist what the patient had discovered about sex and intimacy during the early stages of therapy so that the patient could be sure of making it work "in real life"). The sexual relationship was also claimed to help the patient develop—under the watchful eye of the therapist—a healthier view of his or her own sexuality and a more varied and complete array of sexual responses; sexually corrective experiences that would help the patient recover from dysfunction caused by prior sexual trauma; and the opportunity to overcome a disabling "mind-body" split in which the patient's reactions were overly intellectualized.

One difficulty the proponents of this view experienced was that mention of the dual relationship — supposedly a key component of the treatment plan — was often absent from any part of the chart notes or informed consent procedures. Therapists had difficulty explaining why, if they had carefully considered how a dual relationship was the treatment of choice and had implemented it carefully, they had neglected to obtain the patient's informed consent for the procedure and why they failed to note the consideration or use of the treatment strategy in the chart notes.

A second problem faced by those who sought to justify their behavior to the civil courts, licensing boards, and ethics committees was their difficulty finding substantial research evidence that implementing dual relationship treatment was a safe and effective way to produce positive therapeutic change. Such research was exceedingly rare. Perhaps the most frequently cited exception was the study of 1,500 cases of therapist-patient sexual intimacy, each supposedly benefiting the patient, reported by McCartney (1966). McCartney maintained that engaging in sexual dual relationships must be done in an exceptionally careful manner with scrupulous attention to all ethical aspects, an approach that is still frequently echoed today by those who would defend sexual or nonsexual dual relationships. The therapist, for example, must be certain that he or she is free from any self-serving or self-interested motives. In all cases the patient's welfare must be protected. McCartney's approach and the conclusions he drew from the 1,500 patients, however, were not persuasive to most therapists, or to most courts, licensing boards, or ethics committees.

Some therapists acknowledged that there was virtually no research evidence or other systematic data supporting the hypothesis that dual relationships are a safe and effective method to produce therapeutic change. They maintained that their implementation of the dual relationship was on a trial basis, as part of a research or quasi-research effort to obtain just such evidence. However, it was often difficult for these therapists to establish that they had provided adequate procedural safeguards (such as informed consent) to the patients on whom this experimental method was being tested (see Levine, 1988; Pope, 1990b, 1990c).

Prevalence. Therapists may attempt to justify engaging in dual relationships with their patients by asserting that many other therapists engage in the practice. In some instances, this assertion is carelessly made and seems little more than the frequent claim of those in the public eye who cannot find other means to justify less-than-savory behavior: "Everybody does it!" But in other cases, it is a carefully crafted and articulated attempt to establish the legitimacy and acceptability of a behavior because at least a "sizable minority" of the professional community engage in it. Such a defense is often effective in malpractice trials. The professional need establish not that the method he or she used is generally accepted by peers but only that a sizable or "respectable" minority endorse the procedure. This approach was used in some of the early malpractice trials in which therapists who acknowledged engaging in sexual dual relationships with their patients emphasized that the early surveys of therapist-patient sexual intimacies (for example, Holroyd & Brodsky, 1977) indicated that around 10 percent of male therapists reported engaging in sexual relationships with their patients. This 10 percent figure, acording to the defense, represented a sizable minority of the professional community who accepted and endorsed, via their own behavior with patients, the legitimacy of therapist-patient sexual relations.

The reflexive acceptance of the "prevalence" argument may have encouraged or facilitated both sexual and nonsexual dual relationships. But the argument itself does not seem to address the issue of whether dual relationships are indeed a safe and effective way to produce beneficial change in the patient. Various behaviors that may be unethical, illegal, or clinically contraindicated may unfortunately be practiced, from time to time, by a sizable minority and sometimes even a majority of the professional community. National surveys of therapists have indicated, for example, that over 20 percent of the participants have rendered clinical services for which they (by their own judgment) were clearly incompetent, over 20 percent intentionally breached their patient's legal right to confidentiality, a majority performed clinical work when they were so distressed that they were unable to function effectively, and a majority breached their patient's legal right to confidentiality through negligence (Pope & Bajt, 1988; Pope, Tabachnick & Keith-Spiegel, 1987). The fact that a substantial number of professionals engage in a practice does not, in and of itself, indicate whether the practice is ethical, legal, safe, or effective.

Tradition. Some dual relationships are created through an exchange of services. For example, the therapist provides psychotherapy to the patient; in exchange, the patient does typing and filing for the therapist, creates a painting to decorate the therapist's waiting room, or provides child care for the therapist's sons and daughters. Therapists who develop this kind of dual relationship with their patients often assume that the practice is ethical and not harmful because bartering has a rich historical tradition.

The problem for this justification is that the tradition of service bartering in early American life and culture did not include psychotherapy. Attempts to assert that psychotherapy is functionally equivalent to those services that have traditionally been the subject of bartering ignore the context. Nearly any practice such as bartering may be not only sensible and safe but also socially beneficial in certain forms of exchange and may indicate no harm or risks in the abstract. In virtually all cases, however, the context is crucial. Thus the tradition of giving gifts may be a wonderful one; giving an expensive gift to a judge who is trying a case in which one is a principle participant is frowned upon. The tradition of passionate sexual relationships may be treasured by many; such relationships, when they involve therapist and patient, can be disastrous. The professional or psychotherapeutic context cannot be ignored.

Client Autonomy. Sexual and nonsexual dual relationships are often rationalized by reflexively asserting the concept of "client autonomy." This concept becomes a cloak for unethical behavior; it appears to refer to a client's right that is so fundamental, absolute, and unquestionable that no other consideration could possibly intervene.

The basic premise is that if the client desires a sexual or nonsexual dual relationship with a therapist, whether before or after termination, the therapist has no right — let alone responsibility — to refuse because to do so would interfere with the client's autonomy. Thus ethical, professional, and similar prohibitions against harmful behaviors must be set aside, according to this argument, if they threaten the fundamental value of client autonomy.

Such arguments tend to appear merely as assertions, rather than in the context of coherent ethical and clinical theory. But perhaps most striking is their proponents' failure to apply the concept to other areas of practice. For example, for a nonmedical therapist (one neither trained nor licensed to prescribe medication) to provide drugs to a client would put that client at risk. Yet what if a client begged his or her nonmedical therapist to personally provide drugs? An ethical therapist would respectfully but firmly decline, explaining the reasons for declining and exploring options such as referral to a physician. An ethical nonmedical therapist would *not* invoke the concept of the client's inviolable autonomy as a rationalization to provide the client with drugs.

As another example, if a client or former client wanted to take up residence in the therapist's waiting room, the therapist would not agree to such an arrangement to avoid interfering with the client's autonomy.

Proponents' inconsistent use of the concept of client autonomy (or other superficial rationalizations such as "right to assemble") reveals the degree to which the actual meaning of this concept has been taken out of concept and misused in service of the therapist's desire to engage in sex (or in some other dual relationship) with someone to whom he or she has agreed to provide professional services.

Necessity. Dual relationships may be accepted with virtually no ethical or clinical scrutiny when they are asserted to be "necessary." The therapist claims that there was no alternative but to engage in a dual relationship. The therapist using this justification refuses to accept any responsibility for entering a dual relationship; the therapist must simply accept what is determined by forces beyond his or her control. Thus dual relationships may be termed "inevitable" or "unavoidable."

Yet the "my hands were tied" approach may represent a combination of a failure to explore and create alternative approaches that meet the highest clinical, legal, and ethical standards and an unsubtle attempt to evade responsibility. Careful, determined, imaginative attempts to meet the needs of patients without resorting to sexual or nonsexual dual relationships can overcome the rationalization of necessity. Michael Enright, for example, discussed the dilemma of therapists in a very small town in which the hospital administration called for a periodic review of all current patients (personal communication, May 13, 1989). The therapists at the hospital were to conduct this review. The problem it presented is obvious: Although they had scrupulously avoided treating patients with whom they had other ongoing (social or business) relationships, the therapists would, by conducting this periodic review of all cases, become aware of diagnostic and treatment issues as well as other "private" information about their friends and business associates. Enright pointed out that among a whole tangle of ethical and clinical issues is that of informed consent: The patients did not understand that their social and business associates would be reviewing their course of treatment nor had they consented to such a review. Examination of these issues led to the idea that a clinician from a different community could be brought in on a regular basis both to review current cases and to ensure that all patients adequately understood and consented to the review process.

Conclusion

The harm and exploitation that results from both sexual and nonsexual dual relationships is perpetrated overwhelmingly by male professionals on an overwhelmingly female patient population, a pattern that may have played a role in our difficulty addressing this issue vigorously and effectively. The initial research has led to specific recommendations for education and training (Borys & Pope, 1989), but much remains to be done. The vulnerability of individuals who are seeking help from a therapist and the harm that is done both to the welfare of the patient and to the integrity of the profession when the role of therapist is abused makes it extremely hard to justify further neglect of the issue in our research, writings, and professional efforts to ensure the highest level of ethical and clinical practice.

It is crucial to clarify our relationship to each patient and to avoid sexual and nonsexual dual relationships which prevent that clarity and place the patient at great risk for harm. Achieving that clarity is impossible without adequate awareness and appreciation of cultural, contextual, and individual differences—the subject of the next chapter.

11

Cultural, Contextual, and Individual Differences

Our society's cultural diversity and broad range of social classes have important ethical implications for counselors and psychotherapists. Differences in cultural background or social class between clinician and client can create needless barriers to the delivery of effective services by the ethically unaware, unprepared, or careless clinician.

One of the major responsibilities is twofold. On the one hand, the clinician must become adequately knowledgeable and respectful of the client's relevant cultural or socioeconomic contexts. Therapists who ignore cultural values, attitudes, and behaviors different from their own deprive themselves of crucial information and may tend to impose their own worldview and assumptions upon clients in an exceptionally fallacious and destructive manner. On the other hand, the clinician must avoid making simplistic, unfounded assumptions on the basis of cultural or socioeconomic contexts. Knowledge about cultural and socioeconomic contexts becomes the basis for informed inquiry rather than the illusion of uniform group characteristics with which to stereotype the client. Neither variation between groups nor within groups can be discounted or ignored.

Some readers may object to the apparent restriction of this twofold ethical responsibility to clinical situations in which the clinician and client are of different cultural or socioeconomic backgrounds. They might argue that the need to understand any client's background or context and to avoid assuming that the individual can somehow be "summarized" by certain group characteristics are essential ethical responsibilities in any clinical endeavor. They would be emphasizing an important point. As Pedersen, Draguns, Lonner, and Trimble (1989, p. 1) emphasize in *Counseling Across Cultures:* "Multicultural counseling is not an exotic topic that applies to remote regions, but is the heart and core of good counseling with any client."

Our training, however, often fails to teach us how to apply the basic principles of counseling beyond the values and ethos of the majority culture. In our society, furthermore, culture, race, ethnicity, socioeconomic status, and related factors of "difference" are frequently emotion-laden concepts that may inhibit, distort, or diminish rather than enrich the caring and trust necessary to an effective therapeutic process (see Chapter Three). Similarly, the differential power between therapist and client (see Chapter Three) may lose its enabling, healing, or therapeutic force and become instead a reflection of the power differential that is frequently perceived between the rich and the poor, between the racial majority and minorities, and between other social, economic, or political groupings. For such reasons, a chapter focusing on issues of cultural, socioeconomic, and similar differences seems useful and warranted, even though it will address some of the same topic areas — competence and assessment, for example — explored in other chapters. The purpose is not only to identify some of the barriers to fulfilling our ethical responsibilities in regard to these forms of "difference" (and by implication or analogy, to other forms of difference) but also to note effective approaches to transcending these barriers.

Acknowledging Socioeconomic Differences

One of the initial steps in an ethical approach to the issue of difference is simply an awareness of the great socioeconomic differences that exist in our society. It is exceptionally easy for us to create a cognitive map of the world in which over 90 percent of the area is represented by our own immediate environment. We lose active awareness that many people live in significantly different contexts. We minimize the differences and forget the contrasts and their implications. One vivid example of the extreme conditions in which some U.S. citizens live was provided by the epidemiological study of New York published in the *New England Journal of Medicine* (McCord & Freeman, 1990). The analysis showed that 54 of the 353 health areas in New York had at least double the anticipated mortality rate for individuals under sixty-five years old. With only one exception, all of these 54 areas were predominantly African-American or Hispanic. "Survival analysis showed that black men in Harlem were less likely to reach the age of 65 than men in Bangladesh" (p. 173). The authors pointed out that their findings were similar to those for natural disaster areas.

What does it mean to us as therapists and counselors that fellow citizens live in such conditions? At a minimum, it requires that we acknowledge the reality of such conditions and that we inform ourselves adequately when we provide professional services to those from such lethal conditions or from other distinct contexts that differ from our own.

But such conditions also confront us with inescapable ethical questions regarding the degree to which we as individuals and as a profession view ourselves as responsible in some part for addressing these conditions, regardless of whether circumstances bring clients from those conditions to our offices. Goodyear and Sinnett (1984), for example, are among those who argue that counselors and therapists have an ethical responsibility to work to protect client populations against harm imposed by oppressive systems. Such work might include advocating against agency policies that have a deleterious effect on ethnic minority clients or to developing preventive and developmental interventions as strategies to enhance the quality of life for ethnic minorities (Casas & Vasquez, 1989).

Remaining Alert to Possible Bias
in Interpreting Research

A second step in an ethical approach to the issue of difference is to remain alert to the tendency for group differences to form a basis for stereotyping, bias, and discrimination whether based on factors of race, culture, gender, religions, physical disability, geography, or socioeconomics. The extent to which our vulnerability to such prejudice can shape our interpretation of "scientific" research is illustrated by a carefully planned study by Bache (1894). Conducting his research (in collaboration with Professor Lightner Witmer) at the University of Pennsylvania using finely calibrated, state-of-the-art magnetoelectric apparatus, Bache was concerned with both gender-based and racially based differences in reaction time, or "automatic movements."

Bache was convinced that men would have faster reaction times than women and that this would prove the intellectual (and perhaps overall) superiority of men. Moreover, Bache was convinced that the "Caucasian Race" would manifest faster reaction times than both the "Indian Race" and the "African Race."

The first set of experiments focused on differences between men and women. The men had faster reaction times than the women, leading Bache to conclude that men were intellectually superior: "The reaction time of women, as settled by the same indisputable method, was . . . determined as less than that of men, and this result, it will be observed, is in strict accordance with the fact that the brain development of men, as compared with that of women, is greater, even when taking into account the relatively greater weight of normal individuals of the male sex as compared with that of normal individuals of the opposite one" (p. 482).

When he conducted the research into racial differences, he was surprised. "The first thing that strikes one, upon examination of the tables, is the relative slowness of the Whites, as compared with the Indians and Africans" (p. 484). These results led Bache to conclude that the Whites were intellectually superior to the Indians and Africans! Despite his prior analysis of male-female differences (in which faster reaction times indicated intellectual superiority), Bache reasoned that the White "intellectuality [had] been gained at the expense of his automatic capacity" (p. 480). Thus, the advancement of the intellect had caused, "through the law of compensation" (p. 480), a slowing down of reflexes.

In other words, doing well on a test that had been set forth as positively correlated with intelligence (based on purported faster reaction times for men in comparison with women) was interpreted as proof of inferior intellect: "That the negro is, in the truest sense, a race inferior to that of the white can be proved by many facts, and among these by the quickness of his automatic movements as compared with those of the white" (p. 481). Reviews of more recent research and assessment stretegies indicate that such bias has been, unfortunately, a continuing problem (see, for example, Block & Dworkin, 1976; Cole & Bruner, 1972; Geller, 1988; Gibbs & Huang, 1989; Gossett, 1963; Gould, 1981; E. E. Jones & S. J. Korchin, 1982; J. M. Jones, 1990a, 1990b; J. M. Jones & C. Block, 1984; Murphy, 1976; Ridley, 1989; Scarr & Weinberg, 1976; Stanton, 1960; Thomas & Sillen, 1972).

Potential Problems with Assessment Instruments

A third useful step in confronting ethically the issue of difference is to remain alert to the possibility that standardized tests and other assessment instruments may manifest bias. LaFromboise and Foster (1989), for example, discuss the case of *Larry P. v. Riles* in which the intelligence testing that led to the placement of an African-American student into a special education class was unlawful because of the bias of the tests used. They describe two instruments that were specifically developed to avoid racial or cultural bias in assessment of abilities: The Adaptive Behavior Scale (American Association on Mental Deficiency, 1974) and the System of Multicultural Pluralistic Assessment (Mercer, 1979).

An example of a standardized personality test that has been called into question in regard to potential bias is the original Minnesota Multiphasic Personality Inventory (MMPI; not the revised MMPI-2). African Americans, Native Americans, Hispanics, and Asian Americans were among the groups omitted from the sample from which the original MMPI norms were developed. What implications does this exclusion have for the ethical use of the test? Faschingbauer (1979, p. 385) vividly described his reservations: "The original Minnesota group seems to be an inappropriate reference group for the 1980s. The median individual in that group had an eighth-grade education, was married, lived in a small town or on a farm, and was employed as a lower level clerk or skilled tradesman. None was under 16 or over 65 years of age, and all were white. As a clinician I find it difficult to justify comparing anyone to such a dated group. When the person is 14 years old, Chicano, and lives in Houston's poor fifth ward, use of original norms seems sinful."

A former president of the APA Division of the Society for Personality Assessment, Erdberg (1988) reported that in one research study, a single item from the original MMPI discriminated perfectly on the basis of race, that is to say, it differentiated all African-American test takers from all Caucasian test takers in this rural community.

Potential Problems with the Interaction Process

Whether we are conducting an assessment or are conducting therapy or counseling, our interaction with the client is obviously of great significance. J. M. Jones (1990b) reviewed a variety of research studies demonstrating the degree to which such factors as race could, if not addressed carefully, undermine the process. For example, failing to take such factors into account can contribute to a high premature dropout rate for minorities seeking mental health services.

One set of studies conducted by Word, Zanna, and Cooper (1974; reviewed by J. M. Jones, 1990b) demonstrates the degree to which subtle, unintentional discrimination by the individual conducting the assessment can lead to impaired performance by the person being assessed. In the first part of the study, white interviewers asked questions of both white and African-American individuals. There were significant differences in interviewer behavior. Those conducting the assessment spent more time with the white interviewees, looked directly at white interviewees a greater portion of the time, maintained less physical distance from white interviewees, and made fewer speech errors with white interviewees.

For the second part of the study, white interviewers were trained to become aware of and to use both styles of interview. They were then asked to interview a number of white people. With half of the white interviewees, the interviewer conducted the interview in a style consistent for white interviewees (for example, a longer interview at less distance). With the other half of the white interviewees, the interviewer followed a style consistent for black interviewees (shorter interview, more distance). The latter interviewees performed much less well on a series of objective measures during the assessment interview. Thus even if the tests or assessment instruments themselves are relatively free of bias, the behavior of the interviewer can influence those who are being assessed in a discriminatory way that impairs performance.

Understanding the Context

Addressing the issue of difference involves more than acknowledging important differences and avoiding prejudice and stereotyping; it involves an active appreciation of the context in which clients live and understand their lives. Westermeyer (1987, pp. 471–472) provides an example of this appreciation.

A 48 year old ethnic Chinese woman had been receiving antipsychotic and antidepressant medication for psychotic depression. On this regimen, the patient had lost even more weight and more hope and had become more immobilized. A critical element in this diagnosis of psychosis was the woman's belief that her deceased mother, who had been appearing in her dreams, had traveled from the place of the dead to induce the patient's own death and to bring her to the next world. We interpreted this symptom not as a delusional belief but as a culturally consistent belief in a depressed woman who had recently begun to see her deceased mother in her dreams (a common harbinger of death in the dreams of some Asian patients). This patient responded well after the antipsychotic medication was discontinued, the antidepressant medication was reduced in dosage, and weekly psychotherapy was instituted.

Similarly, the research of Amaro, Russo, and Johnson (1987) demonstrates the importance of an attentive and informed appreciation of different contexts. In comparing sources of strength and stress for Hispanic and Anglo female professionals, they found similar family and work characteristics to be associated with positive mental health. Income was the most consistently related demographic factor across all measures of psychological well-being. In addition, however, Hispanic women's psychological well-being was related to the experience of discrimination, which was reported by more than 82 percent of the sample. Those of us who are not subject to discrimination in our day-to-day lives may find it easy to misinterpret and mistreat the distress and dysfunction that can result from prejudice.

Creativity

A final step to be mentioned in this discussion of differences involves a creative and thorough approach to human diversity. In a careful series of studies at Harvard University, Langer, Bashner, and Chanowitz (1985) asked children to consider individuals who were different from the mainstream in that they were physically challenged. In one study, the experimental group of children were asked to think of as many ways as possible that a disabled person might meet a particular challenge while the control group children were simply asked if the disabled person could meet the challenge. For example, children were shown a picture of a woman in a wheelchair and were asked either *how* the woman could drive a car or *whether* the woman could drive a car. In another study, children in the experimental group were asked to give numerous reasons not only why a handicapped individual—a blind person, for example—might be bad at a particular profession but also why he or she might be good at it.

In these and other studies, Langer (1989) found that creativity in responding to forms of human difference can indeed be taught and that it can lead to more realistic, less prejudiced reactions to individuals who differ in some way from the mainstream. The research showed "that children can be taught that handicaps are function-specific and not person-specific.

Those given training in making mindful distinctions learned to be discriminating without prejudice. This group was also less likely than the control group to avoid a handicapped person. In essence, the children were taught that attributes are relative and not absolute, that whether or not something is a disability depends on context" (pp. 169–170).

Whether we practice in private offices, hospitals, clinics, community mental health centers, university settings, or elsewhere, we must remain alert and creative in regard to the contexts in which we work and the characteristics of those who need our help. Is our setting responsive to the needs of those who use wheelchairs, those for whom English is a new language, those who use American Sign language to communicate, or those who are blind? For whom is our setting open, inviting, accessible, and genuinely helpful? Who is shut out or discouraged from approaching? To what degree do we acknowledge or assume responsibility for the nature of the settings in which we practice?

12

Maintaining and Waiving Confidentiality

Ethics complaints, malpractice suits, and licensing disciplinary actions make clear the difficulties most of us encounter in addressing issues of confidentiality (see Chapter Two). A five-year study of ethics complaints resulting in disciplinary actions against psychologists found that violation of Principle 5a (failing to preserve appropriate confidentiality of information concerning clients, students, and so on) was the fourth most frequent basis of disciplinary action (Ethics Committee of the APA, 1988b). An examination of malpractice suits closed during a twelve-year period found that breach of confidentiality accounted for 6.4 percent of the total claims against psychologists covered under the APA's professional liability policy (Pope, 1989a). Finally, confidentiality was an issue noted as a basis for disciplinary actions taken against psychologists by state licensing boards (Pope, 1989a).

Frequencies of formal complaints or disciplinary actions may significantly underestimate the scope of the problem. Over half (61.9 percent) of the psychologists responding in one national study reported *unintentionally* violating their patients' confidences (Pope, Tabachnick & Keith-Spiegel, 1987). Another national study found that the most frequently reported *intentional* violation of the law or ethical standards by senior, prominent psychologists involved confidentiality (Pope & Bajt, 1988). In

21 percent of the cases, psychologists violated confidentiality in transgression of law. In another 21 percent of the cases, psychologists refused to breach confidentiality to make legally required reports of child abuse.

Because each state differs from the others in terms of applicable legislation, case law, and administrative licensing regulations, there is considerable variation in the ways in which the distinct (but interrelated) issues of privacy, confidentiality, and privilege as well as mandatory or discretionary reporting authorizations are defined.

This chapter will highlight twenty aspects of clinical work in which therapists and counselors frequently run afoul of ethical or legal standards.

Written Consent

Perhaps one of the most frequent errors that psychologists make regarding consent for releasing confidential information is to fail to obtain informed consent *in writing*. The "General Guidelines for Providers of Psychological Services" (APA, 1987b) emphasizes that, unless authorized otherwise by law, "Psychologists do not release confidential information, except with the written consent of the user involved, or of his or her legal representative, guardian, or other holder of the privilege on behalf of the user, and only after the user has been assisted to understand the implications of the release" (p. 717).

Divulging Confidential Information Only to the Extent Required by Law

It is crucial that therapists remain aware of evolving legislation and case law regarding how much information is to be disclosed in making legally mandated reports. As an example, a psychologist was contacted by a mother who wished to arrange appointments for her daughter and her daughter's stepfather to see the therapist regarding allegations that the stepfather engaged in sexual intimacies with his stepdaughter. The psychologist agreed to meet with them and immediately filed a formal report of suspected child abuse. The next day, a deputy sheriff contacted the psychologist for information. The psychologist furnished information concerning his meeting with the daughter. He would meet with the stepfather later in the day. The deputy called later and asked for information concerning the session with the stepfather and, reading from the Child Abuse Reporting Law, emphasized that the psychologist was obligated to supply additional information, which the psychologist reluctantly provided.

The stepfather claimed in court that the psychologist, after making the initial formal report, should not have disclosed any additional information. The Supreme Court of California agreed with the stepfather: "[The psychologist] was under no statutory obligation to make a second report concerning the same activity. . . . We have recognized the contemporary value of the psychiatric [sic] profession, and its potential for the relief of emotional disturbances and of the inevitable tensions produced in our modern, complex society. . . . That value is bottomed on a confidential relationship; but the doctor can be of assistance only if the patient may freely relate his thoughts and actions, his fears and fantasies, his strengths and weaknesses, in a completely uninhibited manner" (*People v. Stritzinger*, 1983, p. 437).

In some cases, therapists who disclose confidential information *even in court settings* may be subject to suit by the patient. California, for example, has general legislation protecting individuals from lawsuits for any statements made as part of court proceedings. Nevertheless, a district court of appeal ruled that a psychologist "can be sued for disclosing privileged information in a court proceeding when it violates the patient's constitutional right of privacy" (Chiang, 1986, p. 1).

Client Comprehension of the Limitations of Privacy, Confidentiality, and Privilege

A patient should understand *in advance* the circumstances under which the therapist is required or allowed to communicate information about the patient to third parties. Without such understanding, the patient's consent to treatment is not genuinely informed. Therapists need to clarify what their ethical and legal obligations are to patients in this regard (according to legislation and case law applicable in their state). The clinical implications of withholding this information from patients also need to be considered. As one appeal court judge wrote in consideration of the patient's lack of privilege regarding disclosure of child abuse, "In order to protect a patient's expectation of privacy regarding the seemingly therapeutic and confidential therapy session, however, the therapist should warn the patient of his or her statutory duty to testify against the patient, concerning instances of child abuse" (*People v. Younghanz*, 1984, p. 911).

Insurance Forms

Clients may not adequately understand the type of information that insurance companies require to authorize coverage and the degree to which information will or will not be sufficiently safeguarded by the insurance company. Keith-Spiegel and Koocher (1985) describe a hypothetical example of a therapist's routine statement to patients regarding insurance coverage: "If you choose to use your coverage, I shall have to file a form with the company telling them when our appointments were and what services I performed (i.e., psychotherapy, consultation, or evaluation). I will also have to formulate a diagnosis and advise the company of that. The company claims to keep this information confidential, although I have no control over the information once it leaves this office. If you have questions about this you may wish to check with the company providing the coverage. You may certainly choose to pay for my services out-of-pocket and avoid the use of insurance altogether, if you wish" (p. 76).

A Patient's Writings in Therapy

Occasionally therapists may encourage their patients to keep logs, diaries, or audiorecordings as part of the therapy. Both therapists and patients need to understand clearly the extent to which such materials are—or are not—privileged under state law. For example, in a recent California case, a woman was kidnapped at gunpoint, taken to a deserted location, and raped

(Sahagun, 1988). She sought help from a therapist who specialized in treating victims of sexual assault. The incident was so difficult for the patient to talk about that the therapist suggested she keep a diary of the ideas and emotions she was experiencing. The diary was to be completely private, shared only between patient and therapist. The attorney for the man accused of the rape subpoenaed the diary and supported his demand by reference to a prior district court ruling in a separate case that similar materials must be turned over to the trial judge for review. As the deputy district attorney who was trying the case noted, "The application of this appellate court ruling to this situation means that anything a victim says to a therapist in an attempt to recover from the trauma of being a victim is subject to review in court. . . . That means it would be difficult for victims of crimes to receive the therapy they need" (Sahagun, 1988, p. 43).

Who Is the Client?

In numerous instances, loyalties or responsibilities to third parties or organizations may lead therapists to betray the legitimate or erroneous expectations a patient has regarding confidentiality. In some cases, confusion occurs because a third party—a parent, spouse, or employer—requests the therapist to provide the therapy and in some instances pays the bills. In some cases, confusion occurs because of the setting in which the therapy is conducted—military, forensic, educational. Nevertheless, psychologists have a responsibility to, in the words of the "Ethical Principles" (APA, 1990a), "clarify the nature of the relationships to all parties concerned" (p. 393).

Dyer describes a case in which the betrayal of expected confidentiality had tragic consequences: "At a lecture I gave on confidentiality, a physician in the audience related the following story from his experience as a medical officer during the Korean War: A soldier reported to the infirmary with feelings of depression and an inability to sleep, eat, or concentrate on his work. He said he was upset because his homosexual lover had rejected him. He expressed thoughts of suicide. The physician referred the soldier to a nearby psychiatric unit. There the admitting officer met the soldier, not with the usual offer to help, but with the announcement that this would mean an end to the soldier's military career. Shortly after that the soldier shot and killed himself" (Dyer, 1988, p. 68). Practitioners interested in an extended discussion of these vital issues should read *Who Is the Client?* (Monahan, 1980).

Communications to Psychological Assistants and Interns

Psychologists must clarify whether state law establishes an adequate basis for protecting the confidentiality of patients' communications to unlicensed supervisees and interns. For example, an appeal court in California ruled that the "psychotherapist-patient privilege does not extend to student interns" (*People v. Gomez,* 1982, pp. 158–159). Subsequently, legislation was enacted extending the privilege to such individuals.

Communications in Group or Family Therapy

When treatment encompasses more than one individual, as in group and family therapy, therapists must clarify the extent to which state law provides for the privilege and confidentiality of information obtained in the course of treatment and must furthermore clarify in advance with all parties the extent to which information provided to the therapist by one patient may be shared by the therapist with other patients involved in the treatment. For example, if a clinician is providing family therapy, will he or she keep confidential from other family members information conveyed in a phone call from a minor son that he is using drugs, from a minor daughter that she is pregnant, from the father that he is engaging in an extramarital affair and plans to leave his wife, or from the mother that she has secretly withdrawn the family's savings and is using it to gamble? As another example, a counselor may provide services to a couple who subsequently file for divorce; the counselor may be called to testify by an attorney for one of the clients at a custody hearing.

Case Notes and Patient Files

The "Ethical Principles" (APA, 1990a) provide standards for confidentiality but they do not spell out how confidentiality should be maintained in all settings and situations. What is troubling is that many institutions and individuals fail to guard rigorously the confidentiality of records. In most cases this is unintentional. During a visit to a prestigious university-affiliated teaching hospital, one of the authors noticed, while walking down a public hallway, that the mental health clinic's patient charts were stacked along the walls. The hallway was unattended. The names of the patients were clearly visible, and had the author opened any of the charts, he could have read a wealth of confidential information. When he asked later about charts being left in the hall, he was assured that this was temporary: Due to insufficient funds, additional storage space was not yet available, and this manner of "filing" was most convenient for the business office personnel.

Similarly, some of us may have visited colleagues who leave charts and other patient information lying around on top of their desks. Not only patients' names but also other information may be in full view.

There are at least two important issues here. One is keeping information about clients out of sight of people who are not authorized to see that information. Thus, making sure that documents are inside the chart (or some other protective covering), that the chart folder is closed, and that the client's name does not appear on the outside of the chart (a coding system can provide for convenient filing and retrieval) are useful steps to take when charts are visible in a well-attended area open to the public or other patients). The protection of even the patient's name may seem excessive to some, yet the fact that a person is consulting a mental health professional is a fact worth treating confidentially.

The second important issue concerns the security of charts left in an unattended area. There should be a lock between the charts and anyone not authorized to see those charts. Regarding the security of charts, as in so many aspects of maintaining appropriate confidentiality, the Golden Rule can be a useful guide. What steps would we want a therapist to take if it were our chart, containing our deepest secrets, our personal history, our conflicts, our diagnosis, and our prognosis? What steps would we want our therapist to take to ensure that part or all of this confidential information were not carelessly made available to whoever—other patients, our employer or employees, neighbors, relatives, colleagues—might, for any reason, pass by? How much care would we want our own therapist to use in handling these documents?

Disposing of Charts

In reviewing standards applicable to the disposal of treatment records and other documents related to patients, *The Psychologist's Legal Handbook* (Stromberg et al., 1988) notes that "records should not simply be placed in the trash, since methods of trash collection and disposal can be haphazard and can result in confidential papers being seen by passersby. Instead, records should be shredded and destroyed" (p. 403).

The Specialty Guidelines for the Delivery of Services (APA, 1981) specify that, in the absence of contravening federal, state, or administrative statutes or regulations, APA policy is for clinical psychologists to preserve full records at least three years after termination or the last session, and to preserve either full records or an adequate summary for an additional twelve years. Similarly, counseling psychologists are to keep the full record for at least four years after termination or the last session, and the full record or summary for an additional three years.

Phone Messages

Similar precautions need to be taken with phone messages and other written communications to us regarding patients. Written phone messages taken by a clinic's receptionist should not be left where they can be read by unauthorized individuals. Therapists receiving an emergency call during another patient's session must use exceptional care to ensure that neither patient's privacy is violated.

Answering machines create special pitfalls. It is tempting, if our time for lunch is limited, to play back accumulated messages (some from patients) while a colleague or friend is waiting to accompany us to the nearest restaurant. Similarly, if our answering machine is at home, it may take special measures to ensure that family members, friends, and others do not overhear messages as they are recorded or played back. Again, the Golden Rule can provide a useful guide to anticipating potential problems and to recognizing the importance of providing adequate confidentiality.

Referral Sources

However grateful we may be to colleagues, friends, and others who refer patients to us, such third parties have no inherent right to learn from us whether a specific individual has scheduled an appointment with us, whether or not the individual kept the initial appointment, or what might have been discussed or decided, unless the patient has provided us with written informed consent to provide that information to the referral source (or to any third party). Unfortunately, therapists may unintentionally violate the confidentiality of their patients by sending referral sources a "thank-you" note mentioning a specific patient.

Soundproofing

Confidentiality of assessment or therapeutic sessions cannot be maintained if offices are not adequately soundproofed. Some of us may have had the experience of sitting in a colleague's waiting room, in a clinic's reception area, or in corridors connecting suites of therapy offices and being able to hear what the patient and therapist are discussing.

"Public" Consultation

There are few resources as valuable as consultation to our meeting the highest ethical, legal, and clinical standards. It provides easy access to new information, support, informal "peer review," and a different perspective. In fact, a national study by Pope,

Tabachnick, and Keith-Spiegel (1987) found that for psychologists, consultation with colleagues is the most effective source of guidance for practice; participants in the study rated such consultation as more effective than fourteen other possible sources such as graduate programs, internships, state licensing boards, and continuing education programs (see Chater Five).

Such consultation, however, deserves the same confidentiality as the therapy or other service that is its subject. We lead busy lives and want to make the most of our time. Often the most convenient way to obtain a colleague's advice about the therapy we are conducting is to do so as we are walking through the halls of a clinic, or when we are sitting together at a large table while waiting for the last arrivals so that a meeting can begin, or at a restaurant during a lunch break, or in some other public place. The problem with such "on the run" or ad hoc consultations is that often confidential information is discussed within earshot of people who are not authorized to receive the information. Most of us have probably overheard such consultations in the hallways or elevators of clinics. In some cases we have probably known (socially) the person who was being discussed. In one case (on a crowded elevator), a therapist was consulting a colleague about a particularly "difficult" patient, unaware that the patient was standing only a few feet behind her, listening with intense interest and dismay.

When consulting, taking the time to ensure privacy is an important ethical principle.

Gossip

Few people would argue that therapy is easy work. Sometimes it involves considerable stress, and we need to blow off steam. Occasionally this gives rise to the impulse to talk about our work with others — at parties, in the staff lounge, on the racquetball court. At such times, it is easy to let slip the identity of one of our patients or some other bit of confidential information.

Moreover, some of our patients may be famous or may tell us fascinating information. The urge to let others know of such impressive information may be almost overwhelming at times. Many of us may know "through the grapevine" who is in treatment with whom. To the extent that the information nourishing the grapevine is provided by counselors or therapists rather than by the clients, it is a clear ethical breach.

Publishing Case Studies

Extreme care must be taken whenever material concerning patients is published in the form of case studies or is otherwise publicly presented. Merely changing the patient's name and a few other details may not be sufficient. Pope, Simpson, and Weiner (1978), for example, discussed a case in New York in which a therapist was successfully sued for publishing a book in which he described his treatment of a patient. The patient asserted that the therapist had not obtained her consent to write about her treatment and had not adequately disguised the presentation of her history.

APA's (1987a, p. 72) *Casebook on Ethical Principles of Psychologists* presents a situation in which a psychologist wished to write a book about an assessment.

Psychologist G conducted a professional evaluation of the accused murderer in a sensational and well-publicized case in which six teenage girls, who vanished over a period of 18 months, were later found stabbed to death in an abandoned waterfront area of the city. The lurid nature of the crimes attracted nationwide publicity, which only increased as allegations of negligence were pressed against the city administration and the police force. In order to construct a psychological diagnostic profile, Psychologist G spent several days with the accused, conducting interviews and psychometric tests. He presented his findings in court with the full consent of the accused.

Six months later, following the sentencing of the now convicted murderer, Psychologist G determined that he would like to write a book about the murderer and the psychology behind the crimes, which he anticipated would be a lucrative undertaking. Psychologist G wrote to the Ethics

Committee to inquire whether it would be ethical for him to do so. The convicted murderer had refused permission to publish in a book the results of the psychological evaluation, despite the fact that the information was now considered part of the public domain because it had been admitted in court as evidence.

Opinion: The Ethics Committee responded to Psychologist G that to write the proposed book would be a legal but unethical undertaking. The fact that material has entered the public domain or that there may have been an implied waiver of consent does not free the psychologist from the obligation under Principle 5.b of the Ethical Principles to obtain prior consent before presenting in a public forum personal information acquired through the course of professional work. In this case, the ethics code sets a higher standard than the law would require. Psychologist G thanked the Committee for its advice and dropped the idea of writing the book.

Violations Based on Countertransference

No matter how senior our status, how extensive our training, or how naturally skilled any of us may be, all of us are prone to personal factors that may lead us to violate the confidentiality of our patients. James F. Masterson, a prominent therapist who has written extensively concerning borderline personality disorders, showed courage in writing about an instance in which he betrayed a patient's confidence because of a disconcerting event in his own life: "Sometimes countertransference can arise from the most mundane distractions or preoccupations. One morning I was late and dented my car as I parked in the office garage. A bit frazzled from the experience, I rushed into my office and admitted my first patient who asked me how another patient of mine was doing, calling her by name. I was startled because their appointments were at very different times. I wondered if they had met socially, or if he was dating her. Then I realized what had happened. Worried about my dented fender, I had inadvertently picked her file out of the drawer instead of his, and he had read her name on the folder. My distraction represented a countertransferential failure to pay proper attention to my patient. I apologized for taking out the wrong chart and told him I was distracted by the accident" (Masterson, 1989, p. 26).

Maintaining Confidentiality with Secured Test Materials

In some instances, psychologists have a responsibility to safeguard the confidentiality of test instruments (as distinct from the data those tests produced). This responsibility is noted explicitly in the "Ethical Principles" (APA, 1990a, p. 394): "Psychologists make every effort to maintain the security of tests and other assessment techniques within limits of legal mandates."

A creative approach to establishing a framework in which this responsibility may be fulfilled when conducting forensic work was developed by psychologists and attorneys in New Mexico (W. E. Foote, personal communication, November, 1989). The presidents of the state bar and state psychological association developed a formal statement of principles to which their respective associations formally agreed. The *Statement of Principles Relating to the Responsibilities of Attorneys and Psychologists in Their Interprofessional Relations: An Interdisciplinary Agreement between the New Mexico Bar Association and the New Mexico Psychological Association* (originally drafted by Frank L. Spring, J.D., Ph.D. and William E. Foote, Ph.D.) includes the following section: "Secured instruments, such as Rorschach or TAT cards, testing materials, or other copyrighted materials, should be forwarded only to certified psychologists retained by the requesting attorney" (p. 1).

Deceased Patients

Many psychologists may assume that the death of a patient marks the end of privacy, confidentiality, and/or privilege. Some states, however, have enacted legislation specifically extending the therapist's responsibility to safeguard information regardless of whether the patient is alive. As with all the issues mentioned in this article, practitioners need to remain aware of the evolving legislation and case law applicable in their state.

The Unavailable Therapist

As fallible mortals doing our best to lead our lives, which are frequently unpredictable, we need to take into account our own vulnerabilities and the vicissitudes of life in making arrangements for our records. We may suddenly be called away to provide virtually round-the-clock care for a friend or family member. We may suffer a stroke or be involved in an automobile accident that incapacitates us for a long time, perhaps indefinitely. Without warning, we may, to grab the nearest euphemism, shuffle off this mortal coil. In such cases, have we made adequate preparations so that the appropriate confidentiality of our records will be maintained? Have we provided such arrangements in a way that permits those with a legitimate need for the records — an interim or subsequent therapist for one of our patients — and the appropriate informed consent to gain access to the records without violating the confidentiality of other patients? (See Chapter Six.)

    Access to patient records can be particularly important for clinicians providing coverage in regard to suicidal clients. Information in the record (describing, for example, prior attempts, treatment dynamics, current medications, and prior strategies to handle suicidal impulses or crises) can enable clinicians to respond more knowledgeably and effectively to suicidal risk, the subject of Chapter Thirteen.

13

Responding
to Suicidal Risk

Few responsibilities are so heavy and intimidating for therapists
as carefully assessing and responding to their clients' suicidal
risk. The need for attending to this lethal potential is pressing.
Suicide remains among the top ten causes of death in the United
States, as high as number two for some groups. The high rate
of homicide has seized popular attention and concern, but more
people kill themselves than others. Even psychotherapists limit-
ing their practice to certain highly defined groups are virtually
never free of the responsibility to assess and respond to the risk.
For example, younger people have generally been at lower risk
for suicide, but over the past quarter century the suicide rate
for adolescents has increased two- or threefold. Authorities in
the field are almost unanimous in their view that the reported
figures vastly understate the problem due to difficulties in reporting procedures.

The evaluation and response to suicidal risk is a source
of extraordinary stress for many therapists. This aspect of our
work focuses virtually all of the troublesome issues that run
through this volume: questions of the therapist's influence, competence, efficacy, fallibility, over- or underinvolvement, responsibility, and ability to make life-or-death decisions. Litman's
(1965) study of over 200 clinicians soon after their clients had

committed suicide found the experience to have had an almost nightmarish quality. They tended to have intense feelings of grief, loss, and sometimes depression as anyone — professional or nonprofessional — might at the death of someone they cared about. But they also had feelings associated with their professional role as psychotherapist: guilt, inadequacy, self-blame, and fears of being sued, investigated, or vilified in the media. In a similar study, both the short-term and permanent effects of a client's suicide upon the therapist were so intense that Goldstein and Buongiorno (1984) recommended providing support groups for surviving therapists.

The solo practitioner may be even more vulnerable than his or her colleagues who practice within the contexts of institutions with their natural support systems. Those who are still in training may constitute one of the most vulnerable groups. Kleespies, Smith, and Becker (1990) found that "trainees with patient suicides reported stress levels equivalent to that found in patient samples with bereavement and higher than that found with professional clinicians who had patient suicides" (p. 257). They recommend that all training programs have a protocol for assisting trainees with client suicide: "There is a need for an immediate, supportive response to the student to prevent traumatization and minimize isolation . . . and . . . for a safe forum that will allow the student to express his or her feelings, will ensure positive learning from the experience, and will help the student to integrate it constructively into future work with high-risk patients" (pp. 262–263).

If the challenges of helping the suicidal client evoke extraordinary feelings of discomfort from many therapists, they also serve as the occasion for therapists to take extraordinary measures to help their clients remain alive. Davison and Neale (1982), for instance, describe the ways in which "the clinician treating a suicidal person must be prepared to devote more energy and time than he or she usually does even to psychotic patients. Late-night phone calls and visits to the patient's home may be frequent."

Bruce Danto, a former director of the Detroit Suicide Prevention Center and former president of the American Association of Suicidology, states: "With these problems, you can't simply sit back in your chair, stroke your beard and say, 'All the work is done right here in my office with my magical ears and tongue.' There has to be a time when you shift gears and become an activist. Support may involve helping a patient get a job, attending a graduation or play, visiting a hospital, even making house calls. I would never send somebody to a therapist who has an unlisted phone number. If therapists feel that being available for phone contact is an imposition, then they're in the wrong field or they're treating the wrong patient. They should treat only well people. Once you decide to help somebody, you have to take responsibility down the line" (Colt, 1983, p. 50).

Norman Farberow, one of the preeminent pioneers in the treatment of the suicidal client, described instances in which the therapist provided very frequent and very long sessions (some lasting all day) to a severely suicidal client as "examples of the extraordinary measures which are sometimes required to enable someone to live. Providing this degree of availability to the client gives the client evidence of caring when that caring is absolutely necessary to convince that client that life is both livable and worth living, and nothing less extreme would be effective in communicating the caring. In such circumstances, all other considerations — dependence, transference, countertransference, and so on — become secondary. The overwhelming priority is to help the client stay alive. The secondary issues — put 'on hold' during the crisis — can be directly and effectively addressed once the client is in less danger" (Farberow, 1985, p. C9).

Stone (1982) describes a vivid example of the lengths to which a therapist can go to communicate caring in an effective and therapeutic manner to a client in crisis. Suffering from schizophrenia, a young woman who had been hospitalized during a psychotic episode continuously vilified her therapist for "not caring" about her. Without warning, she escaped from the hospital: "The therapist, upon hearing the news, got into her car and canvassed all the bars and social clubs in Greenwich Village which her patient was known to frequent. At about midnight, she found her patient and drove her back to the hospital. From that day forward, the patient grew calmer, less impulsive, and made great progress in treatment. Later, after making substantial recovery, she told her therapist that all the interpretations during the first few weeks in the hospital meant very little to her. But after the 'midnight rescue mission' it was clear, even to her, how concerned and sincere her therapist had been from the beginning" (p. 171).

Evaluation of Suicidal Risk

Awareness of the following twenty factors may be useful to clinicians evaluating suicidal risk. Four qualifications are particularly important. First, the comments concerning each factor are extremely general, and exceptions are frequent. In many instances, two or more factors may interact. For example, being married and being younger, taken as individual factors, tend to be associated with lower risk for suicide. However, married teenagers show an extremely high suicide rate (Peck & Seiden, 1975). Second, the figures are not static; new research is refining our understanding of the data as well as reflecting apparent changes. The suicide rate for women, for example, has been increasing, bringing it closer to that for men. Third, the list is not comprehensive. Fourth, these factors may be useful as general guidelines but cannot be applied in an unthinking, mechanical, conclusive manner. A given individual may rank in the lowest risk category of each of these factors and nonetheless commit suicide. These factors can legitimately function as aids to, not as substitutes for, a comprehensive, humane, and personal evaluation of suicidal risk. Again it is worth emphasizing a central theme of this volume's approach to ethics: Perhaps the most frequent threat to ethical behavior is the therapist's inattention. Making certain that we consider such factors with each client can help us prevent the ethical lapses that come from neglect.

1. *Direct verbal warning.* A direct statement of intention to commit suicide is one of the most useful single predictors. Take any such statement seriously. Resist the temptation to reflexively dismiss such warnings as "a hysterical bid for attention," "a borderline manipulation," "a clear expression of

negative transference," "an attempt to provoke the therapist," or "yet another grab for power in the interpersonal struggle with the therapist."

2. *Plan.* The presence of a plan increases the risk. The more specific, detailed, lethal, and feasible the plan, the greater the risk.

3. *Past attempts.* Most, and perhaps 80 percent of, completed suicides were preceded by a prior attempt. Schneidman (1976) found that the client group with the greatest suicidal rate were those who had entered into treatment with a history of at least one attempt.

4. *Indirect statements and behavioral signs.* People planning to end their lives may communicate their intent indirectly through their words and actions — for example, talking about "going away," speculating on what death would be like, giving away their most valued possessions, or acquiring lethal instruments.

5. *Depression.* The suicide rate for those with clinical depression is about twenty times greater than for the general population. Guze and Robbins (1970), in a review of seventeen studies concerning death in primary affective disorder, found that fifteen percent of the individuals suffering from this disorder killed themselves.

6. *Hopelessness.* The sense of hopelessness appears to be more closely associated with suicidal intent than any other aspect of depression (Beck, 1990; Beck, Kovaks & Weissman, 1975; Kazdin, 1983; Petrie & Chamberlain, 1983; Wetzel, 1976).

7. *Intoxication.* Between one-fourth and one-third of all suicides are associated with alcohol as a contributing factor; a much higher percentage may be associated with the presence of alcohol (without clear indication of its contribution to the suicidal process and lethal outcome).

8. *Clinical syndromes.* As mentioned earlier, people suffering from depression or alcoholism are at much higher risk for suicide. Other clinical syndromes may also be associated with an increased risk. Kramer, Pollack, Redick, and Locke (1972), for example, found that the highest suicide rates

exist among clients diagnosed as having primary mood disorders and psychoneuroses, with high rates also among those having organic brain syndrome and schizophrenia. Drake, Gates, Cotton, and Whitaker (1984) discovered that those suffering from schizophrenia who had very high internalized standards were at particularly high risk. In a long-term study, Tsuang (1983) found that the suicide rate among the first-degree relatives of schizophrenic and manic-depressive clients was significantly higher than that for a control group of relatives of surgery patients; furthermore, relatives of clients who had committed suicide showed a higher rate than relatives of clients who did not take their lives.

9.   *Sex.* The suicide rate for men is about three times that for women. (For youths, the rate is closer to five to one.) The rate of suicide attempts for women is about three times that for men.

10. *Age.* The risk for suicide tends to increase over the adult life cycle, with the decade from the mid fifties to the mid sixties constituting the age span of highest risk. Attempts by older people are much more likely to be lethal. The ratio of attempts to completed suicides for those up to age sixty-five is about seven to one, but is two to one for those over sixty-five.

11. *Race.* Generally in the United States, Caucasians tend to have one of the highest suicide rates.

12. *Religion.* The suicide rates among Protestants tend to be higher than those among Jews and Catholics.

13. *Living alone.* The risk of suicide tends to be reduced if someone is not living alone, reduced even more if he or she is living with a spouse, and reduced even further if there are children.

14. *Bereavement.* Brunch, Barraclough, Nelson, and Sainsbury (1971) found that 50 percent of those in their sample who had committed suicide had lost their mothers within the last three years (compared with a 20 percent rate among controls matched for age, sex, marital status, and geographic location). Furthermore, 22 percent of the suicides,

compared with only 9 percent of the controls, had experienced the loss of their father within the past five years. Krupnick's (1984) review of studies revealed "a link between childhood bereavement and suicide attempts in adult life," perhaps doubling the risk for depressives who had lost a parent compared to depressives who had not experienced the death of a parent. Klerman and Clayton (1984; see also Beutler, 1985) found that suicide rates are higher among the widowed than the married (especially among elderly men) and that, among women, the suicide rate is not as high for widows as for the divorced or separated.

15. *Unemployment.* Unemployment tends to increase the risk for suicide.

16. *Health status.* Illness and somatic complaints are associated with increased suicidal risk, as are disturbances in patterns of sleeping and eating. Clinicians who are helping people with AIDS, for example, need to be sensitive to this risk (Pope & Morin, 1990).

17. *Impulsivity.* Those with poor impulse control are at increased risk for taking their own lives (Patsiokas, Clum & Luscumb, 1979).

18. *Rigid thinking.* Suicidal individuals often display a rigid, all-or-none way of thinking (Neuringer, 1964). A typical statement might be: "If I don't find work within the next week then the only real alternative is suicide."

19. *Stressful events.* Excessive numbers of undesirable events with negative outcomes have been associated with increased suicidal risk (Cohen-Sander, Berman & King, 1982; Isherwood, Adam & Hornblow, 1982). Some types of recent events may place clients at extremely high risk. For example, Ellis, Atkeson, and Calhoun (1982) found that 52 percent of their sample of multiple-incident victims of sexual assault had attempted suicide.

20. *Release from hospitalization.* Beck (1967, p. 57) has noted that "the available figures clearly indicate that the suicidal risk is greatest during weekend leaves from the hospital and shortly after discharge."

Special Considerations

Coping with the risk that clients may commit suicide creates a special set of responsibilities for the therapist. The themes stressed throughout this book gain exceptional importance and are placed in sharp relief: Failure of the therapist to take necessary steps can literally be fatal for the client. The following steps, which extend or supplement this book's themes, may be helpful in identifying and coping with the chance that a client may be at risk for suicide.

1. *Screen all clients for suicidal risk during initial contact and remain alert to this issue throughout the therapy.* Even clients who are seriously thinking of taking their own life may not present the classic picture of agitated depression or openly grim determination that is stereotypically (and sometimes falsely) portrayed as characteristic of the suicidal individual. In some cases the suicidal client may seem, during initial sessions, calm, composed, and concerned with a seemingly minor presenting problem. Clients who may in fact not be suicidal during initial sessions and who may actually have sought therapy to help them cope with a relatively minor problem may, during the course of therapy, become suicidal. The increase in suicidal risk may be due to external events, such as the loss of a job or a loved one, or to internal events, such as setting aside psychological defenses or discovering traumatic incidents—for example, incest—that had been repressed. What is crucial is that the therapist must not neglect an adequate assessment of the client's suicidal potential at adequate intervals. In some cases, comprehensive psychological testing or the use of standardized scales developed to evaluate suicidal risk may be useful (see, for example, Beck, Resnick & Lettieri, 1974; Butcher, Graham, Williams & Ben-Porath, 1990; Lettieri, 1982; Neuringer, 1974; Schulyer, 1974; Weisman & Worden, 1972).

2. *Work with the suicidal client to arrange an environment that will not offer easy access to the instruments the client might use to commit suicide.* Suicidal clients who have purchased or focused upon a specific gun or other weapon may agree to place the weapon where they will not have access to it until the crisis or period of greatest risk is over. Suicidal clients who are currently tak-

ing psychotropic or other medication may be planning an overdose. The use of materials prescribed by and associated with mental health professionals may have great symbolic meaning for the client. Arrange that the client does not have access to sufficient quantities of the medication to carry out a suicidal plan.

3. *Work with the client to create an actively supportive environment.* To what extent can family, friends, and other resources such as community agencies and group or family therapy help a suicidal person through a crisis?

4. *While not denying or minimizing the client's problems and desire to die, also recognize and work with the client's strengths and (though temporarily faint) desire to live.*

5. *Make every effort to communicate and justify realistic hope.* Discuss practical approaches to the client's problems.

6. *Consider the use of contracts between therapist and client.* Some suicidal clients will welcome such contracts in which the client agrees either to refrain from suicide (at least for a given time — sometimes only until the next session) or to take certain steps such as contacting the therapist before making a suicide attempt. Other clients may initially resist but gradually, grudgingly agree to a contract. Regardless of the client's attitude when the contract is made (and there is, of course, no way to "enforce" such a contract), the contract may give the client a psychological reason to resist an otherwise overwhelming suicidal impulse.

7. *Explore any fantasies the client may have regarding suicide.* Reevaluating unrealistic beliefs about what suicide will and will not accomplish can be an important step for clients attempting to remain alive.

8. *Ensure clear communication and evaluate the probable impact of any interventions.* Ambiguous or confusing messages are unlikely to be helpful and may cause considerable harm. The literature documents the hazards of using such techniques as paradoxical intention with suicidal clients. Even well-meant and apparently clear messages may go awry in the stress of crisis. Beck (1967, p. 53) provides an example: "One woman, who was convinced by her psychotherapist that her children needed her even though she believed herself worthless, decided to kill them as well as herself to 'spare them the agony of growing up without a mother.' She subsequently followed through with her plan."

9. *When considering hospitalization as an option, explore the drawbacks as fully as the benefits, the probable long-term and the immediate effects of this intervention.* Farberow (see Colt, 1983, p. 58) warns: "We tend to think we've solved the problem by getting the person into the hospital, but psychiatric hospitals have a suicide rate more than 35 percent greater than in the community."

10. *Be sensitive to negative countertransference and other negative reactions to the client's behavior.* Alan Stone, professor of psychiatry and law at Harvard, has been a pioneer in the acknowledgment of the ways in which some overly fatigued therapists may react with boredom, malice, or even hatred to some suicidal clients. James Chu (quoted by Colt, 1983, p. 56), a psychiatrist in charge of Codman House at McClean Hospital, comments: "When you deal with suicidal people day after day after day, you just get plain tired. You get to the point of feeling, 'All right, get it over with.' " The potential for fatigue, boredom, and negative transference is so great that we must remain constantly alert for signs that we are beginning to experience them. "Maltsberger and Buie discuss therapists' repression of such feelings. A therapist may glance often at his watch, feel drowsy, or daydream — or rationalize referral, premature termination, or hospitalization just to be rid of the patient. (Many studies have detailed the unintentional abandonment of suicidal patients; in a 1967 review of 32 suicides . . . Bloom found 'each . . . was preceded by rejecting behavior by the therapist.') Sometimes, in frustration, a therapist will issue an ultimatum. Maltsberger recalls one who, treating a chronic wrist-cutter, just couldn't stand it, and finally she said, 'If you don't stop that I'll stop treatment.' The patient did it again. She stopped treatment and the patient killed herself" (Colt, 1983, p. 57).

11. *Perhaps most important, communicate caring.* Therapists differ in how they attempt to express this caring. The ways are influenced by the personality, values, beliefs, needs, resources, and immediate situation of the therapist as well as by the personality, resources, immediate and long-term needs, and situation of the client. A therapist (cited by Colt, 1983, p. 60) recounts an influential event early in her career: "I had a slasher my first year in the hospital. She kept cutting herself to ribbons —

with glass, wire, anything she could get her hands on. Nobody could stop her. The nurses were getting very angry . . . I didn't know what to do, but I was getting very upset. So I went to the director, and in my best Harvard Medical School manner began in a very intellectual way to describe the case. To my horror, I couldn't go on, and I began to weep. I couldn't stop. He said, 'I think if you showed the patient what you showed me, I think she'd know you cared.' So I did. I told her that I cared, and that it was distressing to me. She stopped. It was an important lesson." The home visits, the long and frequent sessions, the therapist's late-night search for a runaway client, and other special measures mentioned earlier are ways some therapists have found useful to communicate this caring, although such approaches obviously would not fit all therapists, all clients, or all theoretical orientations. One of the most fundamental aspects of this communication of caring is the therapist's willingness to listen, to take seriously what the client has to say. Farberow (1985, p. C9) puts it well: "If the person is really trying to communicate how unhappy he is, or his particular problems, then you can recognize that one of the most important things is to be able to hear his message. You'd want to say, 'Yes, I hear you. Yes, I recognize that this is a really tough situation. I'll be glad to listen. If I can't do anything, then we'll find someone who can.' "

Avoidable Pitfalls: Advice from Experts

A central theme of this book is that inattention or a lack of awareness is a — if not *the* — most frequent cause for a therapist's violation of his or her clinical responsibilities and of the client's trust. We asked a number of prominent therapists with expertise in identifying and responding to suicidal risk to discuss factors that contribute to therapists' inattention or lack of awareness when working with potentially suicidal clients. Careful attention to these factors can enable therapists to practice more responsively and responsibly.

Norman Farberow, Ph.D., cofounder and former codirector and chief of research at the Los Angeles Suicide Prevention Center, believes that there are four main problem areas. First, therapists tend to feel uncomfortable with the subject; they find it difficult to explore and investigate suicidal risk: "We don't want to hear about it. We discount it. But any indication of risk or intention must be addressed." Second, we must appreciate that each client is a unique person: "Each person becomes suicidal in his or her own framework. The person's point of view is crucial." Third, we tend to forget the preventive factors: "Clinicians run scared at the thought of suicide. They fail to recognize the true resources." Fourth, we fail to consult: "Outside opinion is invaluable."

Erika Fromm, Ph.D., a diplomate in both clinical psychology and clinical hypnosis, is professor emeritus of psychology at the University of Chicago, clinical editor of the *Journal of Clinical and Experimental Hypnosis,* and recipient of the American Psychological Association Division 39 (Psychoanalysis) 1985 Award for Distinguished Contributions to the Field. She states: "Perhaps it's the countertransference or the highly stressful nature of this work, but some clinicians seem reluctant to provide suicidal patients anything more than minimal reassurance. We need to realize that the people who are about to take their own lives are crying out, are communicating their feelings that no one really cares about them. They are crying, in the only way they know how: 'Show me that you really care!' It is so important for us to communicate that we care about them. When my patients are suicidal, I tell them that I care deeply about them and am fond of them. I do everything I can to let them know this."

Jesse Geller, Ph.D., formerly director of the Psychotherapy Division of the Connecticut Mental Health Center, currently maintains a private practice and is director of the Yale University Psychological Services Clinic. He asserts:

> One of the two main problems in treating suicidal patients is our own anger and defensiveness when confronted by someone who does not respond positively — and perhaps appreciatively — to our therapeutic efforts. It can stir up very primitive and childish feelings in us — we can start to feel vengeful, withholding, and spiteful. The key is to become aware of these potential reactions and not to act them out in our relationship with the patient. The other main

problem seems to be more prevalent among beginning therapists. When we are inexperienced, we may be very cowardly regarding the mention of suicide in our initial interviews. We passively wait for the patient to raise the subject and we may unconsciously communicate that the subject is "taboo." If the subject does come up, we avoid using "hot" language such as "murder yourself" or "blow your brains out." Our avoidance of clear and direct communication, our clinging to euphemisms implies to the patient that we are unable to cope with his or her destructive impulses.

Don Hiroto, Ph.D., maintains a private practice, is chief of the Depression Research Laboratory at the Brentwood Veterans Administration Medical Center, and is a former president of the Los Angeles Society of Clinical Psychologists. He believes that a major area of difficulty involves alcohol use: "Alcoholics may constitute the highest risk group for violent death. The potential for suicide among alcoholics is extraordinarily high. At least 85 percent of completed suicides show the presence of at least some level of alcohol in their blood. There are two aspects to the problem for the clinician. First, there is the tendency for us to deny or minimize alcohol consumption as an issue when we assess all of our clients. Second, we are not sufficiently alert to the suicidal risk factors which are especially associated with alcoholics: episodic drinking, impulsivity, increased stress in relationships (especially separation), alienation, and the sense of helplessness."

Larke Nahme Huang, Ph.D., formerly on the faculty of the University of California, Berkeley, is currently an independent research and clinical consultant in the Washington, D.C., area. She stresses the problems involved in treating people with schizophrenia: "Especially as the treatment becomes a matter of years, there's a tendency to become less sensitive, to forget how painful their life can be. This can lead to problems as the clinician sets ever higher goals as the client continues to improve. A client can experience these goals as insufferable pressure. Frequently the client may make a very serious suicide attempt in an effort to escape the pressure. In working with severely disturbed people, clinicians need to utilize hospitalization, especially in times of crisis. Hospital management issues, power struggles, rivalries between professional disciplines, and so on can aggravate the client's crisis. Don't wait until the last minute, when you're in the midst of a crisis, to learn about these realities and to take steps to prevent them from adding to your client's misery."

The late *Helen Block Lewis,* Ph.D., was a diplomate in clinical psychology who maintained a private practice in New York and Connecticut; she also was professor emeritus at Yale University, president of the American Psychological Association Division of Psychoanalysis, and editor of *Psychoanalytic Psychology.* She believed that therapists tend to pay insufficient attention to the shame and guilt their clients experience. For example, clients may experience a sense of shame for needing psychotherapy and for being "needy" in regard to the therapist. The shame often leads to rage, which in turn leads to guilt because the client is not sure if the rage is justified. According to Lewis, the resultant "shame/rage" or "humiliated fury" can be a major factor in client suicides: "Clients may experience this progression of shame-rage-guilt in many aspects of their lives. It is important for the therapist to help the client understand the sequence not only as it might be related to a current incident 'out there' but also as it occurs in the session. Furthermore, it is helpful for clients who are in a frenzied suicidal state to understand that the experience of shame and guilt may represent their attempt to maintain attachments to important people in their lives. Understanding these sequences is important not only for the client but also for the therapist. It is essential that we maintain good feelings for our clients. Sometimes this is difficult when the client is furious, suicidal, and acting out. Our understanding that such feelings and behaviors by a client represent desperate attempts to maintain a connection can help us as therapists to function effectively and remain in touch with our genuine caring for the client."

Ricardo F. Muñoz, Ph.D., is professor of psychology at the University of California, San Francisco; is principal investigator on the N.I.M.H.–funded Depression Prevention Research Project involving English, Spanish, and Chinese-speaking populations; and is coauthor of *Control Your Depression.*

First, clinicians often fail to identify what suicidal clients have that they care about, that they are responsible for, that they can live for. Include animals, campaigns, projects, religious values. Second, inexperienced liberal therapists in particular may fall into the trap of attempting to work out their philosophy regarding the right to die and the rationality or reasonableness of suicide while they are working with a client who is at critical risk. These issues demand careful consideration, but postponing them till the heat of crisis benefits no one. In the same way that we try to convince clients that the darkest hour of a severe depressive episode is not a good time to decide whether to live or die, clinicians must accept that while attempting to keep a seriously suicidal person alive is not a good time to decide complex philosophical questions. Third, don't overestimate your ability to speak someone else's language. Recently, a Spanish-speaking woman, suicidal, came to the emergency room talking of pills. The physician, who spoke limited Spanish, obtained what he thought was her promise not to attempt suicide and sent her back to her halfway house. It was later discovered that she'd been saying that she'd already taken a lethal dose of pills and was trying to get help.

Michael Peck, Ph.D., a diplomate in clinical psychology, maintains a private practice and was a consultant to the Los Angeles Suicide Prevention Center. He observes, "Many therapists fail to consult. Call an experienced clinician or an organization like the L.A. Suicide Prevention Center. Review the situation and get an outside opinion. Therapists may also let a client's improvement (for example, returning to school or work) lull them to sleep. Don't assume that if the mood is brighter, then the suicidal risk is gone." He stresses the importance of keeping adequate notes, including at least the symptoms, the clinician's response, and consultations and inquiries. "There are special issues in treating adolescents," Peck adds. "When they're under sixteen, keep the parents informed. If they are seventeen (when the client, rather than the parents, possesses the privilege) or older but still living with the parents, tell the client that you will breech confidentiality only to save his or her life. In almost every case, the family's cooperation in treatment is of great importance."

Hans Strupp, Ph.D., a diplomate in clinical psychology, is distinguished professor of psychology and director of clinical training at Vanderbilt University. He believes that one of the greatest pitfalls is the failure to assess suicidal potential comprehensively during initial sessions. Another frequent error, he says, is that there too often is a failure to have in place a network of services appropriate for suicidal clients in crisis: "Whether it is an individual private practitioner, a training program run by a university . . . , a small . . . clinic, or [therapists] associated in group practice—there needs to be close and effective collaboration with other mental health professions . . . and with facilities equipped to deal with suicidal emergencies. I'm not talking about pro forma arrangements but a genuine and effective working relationship. In all cases involving suicidal risk, there should be frequent consultation and ready access to appropriate hospitals."

14

The Supervisory
Relationship

This closing chapter addresses supervision not only because it
is a key task for many clinicians but also because supervision
brings into focus so many of the themes running through this
book. All of us began our clinical careers as supervisees. It is
not difficult for us to think of the important ways, some of them
perhaps unintentional, in which our supervisors influenced our
development. The supervisory relationship involves considerable power, trust, and caring, although these factors manifest
themselves in forms different from those in the therapeutic or
counseling relationship.

Clear Tasks, Roles, and Responsibilities

Because supervision involves a minimum of three people—client,
supervisee, and supervisor—relationships and agendas can easily
become confused, sometimes with severely detrimental effects.
The supervisor has an ethical obligation to ensure that the tasks,
roles, and responsibilities are clear. The supervisor, for example, must ensure that the supervisee is neither encouraged nor
allowed to become the supervisor's therapy patient. Some forms
of supervision may share common aspects with some forms of
therapy. Sometimes supervisees, in the course of supervision,

become aware of personal concerns, psychological problems, or behavioral difficulties that might benefit from therapy. If the supervisee decides to seek therapy for these matters, he or she should consult a separate therapist (one with whom the supervisee has no dual relationship).

Although the supervisor has responsibilities both for the care of the client and for the professional growth of the supervisee, the client's welfare must be primary. The supervisor must ensure that no aspect of the training process unduly jeopardizes the client. Supervision frequently occurs within a hospital or clinic, and the therapist-trainees may have predetermined internships or rotations (for example, six months or an academic calendar year). Such time sequences and boundaries must be taken into account when considering the client's welfare. Some clients may be severely damaged if they experience frequent terminations and transfers. Virtually any client will suffer if not informed in advance of the foreseeable end of his or her therapist's period of availability and if such issues are not addressed adequately both in the therapy and in the supervision.

If a therapist-trainee leaves a setting because he or she has become licensed and is ready to practice independently, numerous issues are likely to arise regarding whether the clients are to remain at the training setting (to be assigned to another therapist-trainee) or will follow their original therapist to his or her new practice setting. When such issues are not comprehensively and definitively addressed *at the beginning of training,* problems are likely to arise and the clients may suffer (see, for example, scenario 5 in Chapter One). Occasionally such problems become the basis of lawsuits and ethics complaints (Pope, 1990a).

The supervisor is ultimately responsible—both ethically and legally—for the clinical services that the individuals functioning under his or her supervision provide. Any conflicts between a supervisor and supervisee regarding the best course of treatment must be promptly, honestly, and comprehensively addressed. Both individuals may avoid addressing such conflicts because they are ill-at-ease with conflict itself or authority issues. If conflicts between a supervisor and supervisee are not adequately addressed, it is almost certain that both the supervision and the therapy will suffer. Such conflicts are often acted out or otherwise recreated in the relationship between a supervisee and client. Similarly, the dynamics of the relationship between a supervisee and client are often recreated, acted out, or symbolically represented in the supervisor-supervisee relationship. Such phenomena are like countertransference; they are a customary and normal part of the supervisory process. They are *not* a sign that the therapy is terribly misguided, that the supervisee needs to withdraw from graduate training and seek a line of work that does not involve being around other people, or that the supervisor is an ogre suffering from delusions of adequacy. What they do signal is that important dynamics of the supervisor-supervisee-client triad need to be fully considered, frankly discussed, and sensitively addressed.

Competence

As a complex and significant professional activity, supervision requires the same demonstrable competence that clinical assessment, therapy, and counseling require. "It is vital that the supervisor be well trained, knowledgeable, and skilled in the practice of clinical supervision" (Stoltenberg & Delworth, 1987, p. 175). It would be no more ethical to "improvise" supervision if one lacked education, training, and supervised experience than if one were to improvise hypnotherapy, systematic desensitization, or administration of a Hallstead-Reitan Neuropsychological Test Battery without adequate preparation. As with other aspects of professional work, supervisory knowledge must be continually updated so that the supervision is informed by the evolving research and theory.

In addition to maintaining competence in supervision, the supervising therapist must be competent in the approaches used to assess and treat the client and must ensure that the supervisee is at least minimally competent to provide services to the client. One of the greatest temptations for some supervisors is to form a relationship with a promising supervisee who has had coursework in clinical techniques for which the supervisor may have only superficial or outdated knowledge. Such

supervisors may, if they are not scrupulously careful, find themselves supervising interventions in which they themselves have
no demonstrable competence. Thus a supervisor whose practice is exclusively psychoanalytic and who has not been trained
in cognitive-behavioral techniques may find himself or herself
"supervising" a student employing covert conditioning with a
client; a supervisor whose training and practice are exclusively
in child psychology may unwittingly become supervisor to interventions with older adults; an existential-humanistic counselor who does not use standardized tests may find himself or
herself trying to help a supervisee interpret an MMPI-2 profile.

Assessment and Evaluation

The supervisor must assess continually not only the appropri-
ateness and adequacy of the clinical services provided to the client
but also the professional development of the supervisee. Some
supervisors may be uncomfortable with this significant responsibility.

Supervisees may also be uncomfortable being evaluated,
an issue that needs to be addressed in the supervision. In graduate training programs, internships, arrangements in which supervised hours are being accumulated as a prerequisite to licensure, and many institutional settings, the supervisor's assessment
of the supervisee's strengths, weaknesses, and progress must be
reported to third parties. These reports may profoundly influence
the supervisee's opportunities for continuing in the training program or for future employment.

Supervisors must clearly, frankly, and promptly communicate *to the supervisee* his or her assessment of strengths, weaknesses, and development. Keith-Spiegel and Koocher (1985)
point out that lack of timely feedback is the most common basis of ethics complaints regarding supervision.

In some cases, the supervisor may determine that the supervisee is unable, either temporarily or more permanently, to
conduct clinical work. The supervisor must conscientiously seek
to determine why the supervisee is experiencing difficulties.
Some supervisees may be experiencing intense personal stress

due to overwork, personal loss, or environmental stress. Others may find that doing therapy or counseling has brought to the surface personal conflicts or developmental issues that have not been adequately acknowledged and worked through. Others may experience acute symptoms such as thought disorders, depression, or anxiety to such a degree that they are unable to function effectively. And still others may seem to suffer from relatively long-term developmental or personality disorders.

The supervisor's responsibility is clear and unavoidable in such circumstances. The APA's policy for training programs more generally is also relevant for individual supervisors. The Committee on Accreditation for the American Psychological Association (1989) has stated that all programs "have special responsibility to assess continually the progress of each student" and that "students who exhibit continued serious difficulties and do not function effectively in academic and/or interpersonal situations should be counseled early, made aware of career alternatives, and, if necessary, dropped from the program" (p. B-10).

While supervisors must, when circumstances warrant, ensure that unsuitable and unqualified individuals do not become therapists or counselors—a responsibility we owe to future clients who might be harmed by incompetent or unscrupulous practice—we must also do so in a way that is not unnecessarily hurtful for the supervisee.

Informed Consent

Supervisors have an ethical responsibility to accord appropriate informed consent to both supervisee and client. Supervisees have a right to know how they will be evaluated—what sorts of information the supervisor will use for forming an opinion and what criteria will be used for evaluating that information. They must understand clearly what is expected of them, and what resources are available to them. They need to know to what degree or under what conditions what they reveal to the supervisor will be kept confidential. For example, supervisees may disclose in the course of supervision that they are in therapy, that they are members of a twelve-step program, or that they were abused as children. They must understand clearly whether such information will be shared with third parties.

Clients whose therapists are being supervised also have an ethical right to informed consent to the supervisory arrangements. The first step, of course, is simply to ensure that they know that the clinical services they are receiving are being formally supervised. On January 30, 1984, the APA's Committee on Scientific and Professional Ethics and Conduct (currently termed the Ethics Committee) issued a formal statement regarding ethical standards applicable to supervision. The committee emphasized "that during the onset of a professional relationship with a client, a client should be informed of the psychologist's intended use of supervisors/consultants, and the general nature of the information regarding the case which will be disclosed to the supervisor/consultant. This permits the client to make an informed decision regarding the psychological services with an understanding of the limits of confidentiality attendant to the relationship. Failure to inform the client of such limits violates the patient's confidentiality when the psychologist, without the patient's awareness, discusses the patient/client and his/her diagnosis and treatment or consultation with a supervisor/consultant. The Committee feels that during the onset of a professional relationship with a client/patient, the client/patient should be clearly informed of the limits of confidentiality in that relationship."

In some cases, state laws or regulations may specify the obligation of supervisees to disclose their status. Section 1396.4 of California's Rules of Professional Conduct (Title 16) states: "A psychological assistant shall at all times and under all circumstances identify himself or herself to patients or clients as a psychological assistant to his or her employer or responsible supervisor when engaged in any psychological activity in connection with that employment."

Both supervisor and supervisee have an ethical responsibility to ensure that the client is accurately informed and clearly understands the qualifications and credentials that the supervisee possesses (Pope, 1990a). Clinicians may engage in extensive rationalizations regarding fraudulently presenting supervisees as possessing a level of training that they have not achieved. For example, in many hospital settings, psychological interns may be presented to patients as "Dr. _____" even though they have not yet received a doctorate. Clients have a fundamental right to know whether their therapist possesses a doctorate and whether he or she is licensed to practice independently.

Sexual Issues

Sexual attraction to clients is a common occurrence for psychotherapists (see Chapter Nine). Supervisors have an important ethical responsibility to ensure that the supervisory relationship provides a safe and supportive opportunity to learn to recognize and handle appropriately such feelings. Supervisors also have an important ethical responsibility to ensure that a sexual relationship between supervisor and supervisee does not occur. The APA, for example, currently prohibits on the basis of its "Ethical Principles" (1990a) sexualized dual relationships between clinical supervisors and supervisees: "Romantic or sexually intimate relationships between clinical supervisors and supervisees constitute, by fact and by definition, dual relationships. Psychologists should make every effort to avoid such dual relationships" ("Ethics Update," 1988, p. 36).

A variety of anonymous surveys have attempted to gather information about such intimacies (Glaser & Thorpe, 1986; Harding, Shearn & Kitchener, 1989; Pope, Levenson & Schover, 1979; Robinson & Reid, 1985). The evidence strongly suggests that female trainees, much more than male trainees, are involved in such intimacies, even when data are adjusted for the relative numbers of male and female supervisors and of male and female supervisees. One study found that one out of every four women who had received her doctorate in psychology within the past six years had engaged in sexual intimacies with at least one of her psychology educators (Pope, Levenson & Schover, 1979; see also Pope, 1989b). Glaser and Thorpe (1986) found that in most cases (62 percent), the intimacy occurred either before or during the student's working relationship with the educator.

Supervisors bear the responsibility not only of seeing that such intimacies do not occur but also of ensuring that sexual issues arising in the therapy are addressed frankly, sensitively, and respectfully: "Students need to feel that discussion of their sexual feelings will not be taken as seductive or provocative or as inviting or legitimizing a sexualized relationship with their educators. . . . Educators must display the same frankness, honesty, and integrity regarding sexual attraction that they expect their students to emulate. Psychologists need to acknowledge that they may feel sexual attraction to their students as well as their clients. They need to establish with clarity and maintain with consistency unambiguous ethical and professional standards regarding appropriate and inappropriate handling of these feelings" (Pope, Keith-Spiegel & Tabachnick, 1986, p. 157).

Beginnings and Endings, Absence and Availability

From the beginning of supervision, the supervisee must clearly understand to what degree and under what circumstances the supervisor will be available. If the client has an emergency, does the supervisee know how to reach the supervisor promptly? Will the supervisor be available for phone supervision between the scheduled sessions? Can the supervisor be reached during late-night hours, on weekends, or on holidays? Are there adequate preparations for supervisor absences—both planned and unanticipated? If the supervisor is unavailable during a crisis, does the supervisee have several options for securing necessary help?

As discussed earlier in this chapter, issues regarding the beginning and ending of the supervisory process must be adequately addressed. The termination is likely to elicit from us a variety of feelings. Both supervisor and supervisee may feel tempted to collude in avoiding issues related to the termination of patients. They may also find it easy to avoid issues related to the termination of supervision. If the processs has not gone as well as expected, both supervisor and supervisee may feel frustration, regret, anger, and relief at the prospect that it is all—*finally*—over. Open and honest discussion of how the problems arose and why they were not resolved more effectively may be difficult. If the process has gone well, both may feel joy, pride, and exhilaration, but they may also experience a sense of loss and sorrow that the frequent meetings and shared, intense, productive work are ending.

Such responses should not be denied or neglected. An important aspect of the supervisory process — an aspect that is especially prominent during termination — involves supervisor and supervisee honestly confronting their reactions to each other and to their collaborative work together. What has each gained from the other? In what ways has each surprised, disappointed, angered, or hurt the other? In what ways has the relationship been characterized by interest, attentiveness, support, and creativity? In what ways has it been characterized by dishonesty, betrayal, and stubbornness? How has their relationship been influenced by the setting in which they work? How have power, trust, and caring manifested themselves in the relationship between supervisor and supervisee and during supervision?

The integrity of the supervisory process depends on the degree to which we acknowledge and confront such issues. We begin our clinical work as supervisees and, unless we are exceptionally afraid or uncaring, our growth and development as therapists and counselors continues during our career. If we do not continue in supervision, we must find alternate ways to nurture this process.

We have chosen work that is done in the context of and frequently focuses on intense and intimate relationships with other people. It is work involving great influence but also great vulnerability. Whether our relationships with our clients and supervisees are helpful or hurtful depends to a great extent upon fulfilling our ethical responsibilities in regard to power, trust, and caring.

References

Advice on ethics of billing clients. (1987, November). *APA Monitor,* p. 42.

Amaro, H., Russo, N. F., & Johnson, J. (1987). Family and work predictors of psychological well-being among Hispanic women professionals. *Psychology of Women Quarterly, 11,* 505–522.

American Association for Counseling and Development. (1988). *Ethical standards* (rev. ed.). Alexandria, VA: Author.

American Association for Marriage and Family Therapy. (1988). *Code of professional ethics for marriage and family therapists* (rev. ed.). Washington, DC: Author.

American Association on Mental Deficiency. (1974). *The Adaptive Behavior Scale: Manual.* Washington, DC: Author.

American College Personnel Association. (1989). *A statement of ethical principles and standards* (rev. ed.). Alexandria, VA: Author.

American Psychiatric Association. (1989). *The principles of medical ethics with annotations especially applicable to psychiatry* (rev. ed.). Washington, DC: Author.

American Psychological Association. (1953). *Ethical standards of psychologists.* Washington, DC: Author.

American Psychological Association. (1981). *Specialty guidelines for the delivery of services: clinical psychologists, counseling psychologists, industrial/orgainizational psychologists, school psychologists.* Washington, DC: Author.

American Psychological Association. (1982). *Ethical principles in the conduct of research with human participants.* Washington, DC: Author.

American Psychological Association. (1986). *Guidelines for computer-based tests and interpretations.* Washington, DC: Author.

American Psychological Association. (1987a). *Casebook on ethical principles of psychologists.* Washington, DC: Author.

American Psychological Association. (1987b). General guidelines for providers of psychological services. *American Psychologist, 42,* 712–723.

American Psychological Association. (1987c). *Guidelines for conditions of employment of psychologists.* Washington, DC: Author.

American Psychological Association. (1990a). Ethical principles of psychologists. *American Psychologist, 45,* 390–395.

American Psychological Association. (1990b). *Guidelines for providers of services to ethnically and culturally diverse populations.* Washington, DC: Author.

American Psychological Association Committee on Accreditation (1989). Criteria for accreditation, doctoral training programs and internships in professional psychology (amended version). In *Accreditation handbook* (pp. B-1–B-18). Washington, DC: Author.

American Psychological Association Committee on Ethical Standards for Psychology. (1949). Developing a code of ethics for psychologists. *American Psychologist, 4,* 17.

American Psychological Association Committee on Ethical Standards for Psychology. (1951a). Ethical standards for psychology: Sections 1 and 6. *American Psychologist, 6,* 626–661.

American Psychological Association Committee on Ethical Standards for Psychology. (1951b). Ethical Standards for Psychology: Sections 2, 4, and 5. *American Psychologist, 6,* 427–452.

American Psychological Association Committee on Ethical Standards for Psychology. (1951c). Ethical Standards for Psychology: Section 3. *American Psychologist, 6,* 57–64.

American Psychological Association Insurance Trust. (1990). *Bulletin: Sexual misconduct and professional liability claims.* Washington, DC: Author.

Bache, R. M. (1894). Reaction time with reference to race. *Psychological Review, 1,* 475–486.

Bajt, T. R., & Pope, K. S. (1989). Therapist-patient sexual intimacy involving children and adolescents. *American Psychologist, 44,* 455.

Baker v. United States, 226 F. Supp. 129 (S.D. Iowa 1964).

Bates, C. M., & Brodsky, A. M. (1989). *Sex in the therapy hour: A case of professional incest.* New York: Guilford.

Beck, A. T. (1967). *Depression.* Philadelphia: University of Pennsylvania Press.

Beck, A. T. (1990, August). *Cognitive therapy and cognitive theory: A thirty-year retrospective.* Paper presented at the annual meeting of the American Psychological Association, Boston.

Beck, A. T., Kovaks, M., & Weissman, A. (1975). Hopelessness and suicidal behavior: An overview. *Journal of the American Medical Association, 234,* 1146–1149.

Beck, A. T., Resnick, H. L. P., & Lettieri, D. (Eds.). (1974). *The prediction of suicide.* New York: Charles Press.

Bell, B. E., Raiffa, H., & Tversky, A. (Eds.) (1989). *Decision making: Descriptive, normative, and prescriptive interactions.* Cambridge: Cambridge University Press.

Bellah v. Greenson, 81 Cal. App. 3d 614 (1978).

Benson, P. R. (1984). Informed consent. *Journal of Nervous and Mental Disease, 172,* 642–653.

Beutler, L. E. (1985). Loss and anticipated death: Risk factors in depression. In H. H. Goldman & S. E. Goldston (Eds.), *Preventing stress-related psychiatric disorders* (pp. 177–194). Rockville, MD: National Institute of Mental Health.

Blau, T. H. (1984). *The psychologist as expert witness.* New York: Wiley-Interscience.

Block, N. J., & Dworkin, G. (1976). *The IQ controversy.* New York: Pantheon.

Boice, R., & Myers, P. E. (1987). Which setting is happier: Academe or private practice? *Professional Psychology: Research and Practice, 18,* 526–529.

Borys, D. S. (1988). *Dual relationships between therapist and client: A national survey of clinicians' attitudes and practices.* Unpublished doctoral dissertation, University of California, Los Angeles.

Borys, D. S., & Pope, K. S. (1989). Dual relationships between therapist and client: A national study of psychologists, psychiatrists, and social workers. *Professional Psychology: Research and Practice, 20,* 283–293.

Bouhoutsos, J. C. (1983, August). Programs for distressed colleagues: The California model. Symposium presented at the annual meeting of the American Psychological Association, Anaheim, CA.

Bouhoutsos, J. C., Holroyd, J., Lerman, H., Forer, B., & Greenberg, M. (1983). Sexual intimacy between psychotherapists and patients. *Professional Psychology, 14,* 185–196.

Brodsky, A. M. (1989). Sex between patient and therapist: Psychology's data and response. In G. O. Gabbard (Ed.), *Sexual exploitation in professional relationships* (pp. 15–25). Washington, DC: American Psychiatric Press.

Brown, L. S. (1988). Harmful effects of posttermination sexual and romantic relationships between therapists and their former clients. *Psychotherapy, 25,* 249–255.

Brown, L. S. (1990). Mapping the moral domain: A review and critique. *The Interchange, 8* (2), 5–6.

Brunch, J., Barraclough, B., Nelson, M., & Sainsbury, P. (1971). Suicide following death of parents. *Social Psychiatry, 6,* 193–199.

Burke, E. (1961). *Reflections on the revolution in France.* New York: Doubleday. (Original work published 1790)

Butcher, J. M., Graham, J. R., Williams, C. L., & Ben-Porath, Y. S. (1990). *Development and use of the MMPI-2 content scales.* Minneapolis: University of Minnesota Press.

Butler, S. E., & Zelen, S. L. (1977). Sexual intimacies between therapists and patients. *Psychotherapy, 14,* 139–145.

California Department of Consumer Affairs. (1990). *Professional therapy never includes sex.* (Available from Board of Psychology, 1430 Howe Avenue, Sacramento, CA 95825)

Canterbury v. Spence, 464 F. 2d 772 (D.C. Cir. 1972).

Casas, J. M., & Vasquez, M. J. T. (1989). Counseling the Hispanic client: Theoretical and applied perspectives. In P. D. Pedersen, J. G. Draguns, W. J. Lonner, & E. J. Trimble

(Eds.), *Counseling across cultures* (3rd ed.). (pp. 153–176). Honolulu: University of Hawaii Press.

Cases and inquiries before the Committee on Scientific and Professional Ethics and Conduct. (1954). *American Psychologist, 9,* 806–807.

Cassileth, B. R., Zupkis, R. V., Sutton-Smith, K., & March, V. (1980). Informed consent — Why are its goals imperfectly realized? *New England Journal of Medicine, 323,* 896–900.

Chiang, H. (1986, July 28). Psychotherapist is subject to suit for breaching privilege. *Los Angeles Daily Journal,* p. 1.

Cobbs v. Grant, 502 P.2d 1, 8 Cal.3d. 229 (1972).

Cohen-Sandler, R., Berman, A. L., & King, R. A. (1982). Life stress and symptomotology: Determinants of suicidal behavior in children. *Journal of the American Academy of Child Psychiatry, 21,* 178–186.

Colby, K. (1968). Commentary: Report to the plenary session on psychopharmacology in relation to psychotherapy. In J. M. Schlien (Ed.), *Research in psychotherapy: Vol. 3.* Washington, DC: American Psychological Association.

Cole, M., & Bruner, J. S. (1972). Cultural differences and inferences about psychological processes. *American Psychologist, 26,* 867–876.

Colorado State Board of Medical Examiners v. Weiler, 402 P.2d 606 (1965).

Colorado State Board of Psychology Examiners, Case No. PY88-01 (October 3, 1988).

Colt, G. H. (1983). The enigma of suicide. *Harvard Magazine, 86,* 47–66.

Committee on Professional Standards of the American Psychological Association. (1984). Casebook for providers of psychological services. *American Psychologist, 39,* 663–668.

Cooper v. Board of Medical Examiners, 49 Cal. App. 3d 931, 123 Cal. Rptr. 563 (1975).

Council of Representatives of the American Psychological Association. (1976, January 23–25). Policy on training for psychologists wishing to change their specialty. Minutes of Council meeting.

Council of Representatives of the American Psychological Association. (1982, January 22–24). Respecialization. Minutes of Council meeting.

Court holds bipolar disorder is physical. (1988, March 4). *Psychiatric News,* pp. 1, 16.

Cummings, N. A. (1990). The credentialing of professional psychologists and its implications for the other mental health disciplines. *Journal of Counseling and Development, 5,* 485–491.

Davison, G. C., & Neale, J. M. (1982). *Abnormal psychology: An experimental clinical approach.* New York: Wiley.

Deutsch, C. (1985). A survey of therapists' personal problems and treatment. *Professional Psychology: Research and Practice, 16,* 305–315.

Drake, R., Gates, C., Cotton, P., & Whitaker, A. (1984). Suicide among schizophrenics: Who is at risk? *Journal of Nervous and Mental Disease, 172,* 613–617.

Dyer, A. R. (1988). *Ethics and psychiatry.* Washington, DC: American Psychiatric Press.

Ellis, E. M., Atkeson, B. M., & Calhoun, K. S. (1982). An examination of differences between multiple- and single-incident victims of multiple sexual assault. *Journal of Abnormal Psychology, 91,* 221-224.

Erdberg, P. (1988, August). *How clinicians can achieve competence in testing procedures.* Paper presented at the annual meeting of the American Psychological Association, Atlanta.

Ethics Committee of the American Psychological Association. (1988a, October 5–7). Policy statement.

Ethics Committee of the American Psychological Association. (1988b). Trends in ethics cases, common pitfalls, and published resources. *American Psychologist, 43,* 564–572.

Ethics update. (1988, December). *APA Monitor, 19,* 36.

Evans, J. S. (1989) *Bias in human reasoning.* Hillsdale, NJ: Erlbaum.

Farber, B. A. (1985). Clinical psychologists' perceptions of psychotherapeutic work. *Clinical Psychologist, 38,* 10-13.

Farberow, N. (1985, May 12). How to tell if someone is thinking of suicide. *Los Angeles Herald Examiner,* p. C9.

Faschingbauer, T. R. (1979). The future of the MMPI. In C. S. Newmark (Ed.), *MMPI: Clinical and research trends.* (pp. 380–392). New York: Praeger.

Feldman-Summers, S. (1989). Sexual contact in fiduciary relationships. In G. O. Gabbard (Ed.), *Sexual exploitation in professional relationships* (pp. 193–209). Washington, DC: American Psychiatric Press.

Feldman-Summers, S., & Jones, G. (1984). Psychological impacts of sexual contact between therapists or other health care professionals and their clients. *Journal of Consulting and Clinical Psychology, 52,* 1054–1061.

Fernberger, S. W. (1932). The American Psychological Association: A historical summary, 1892–1930. *Psychological Bulletin, 31,* 1–89.

Fink, P. J. (1989). Presidential address: On being ethical in an unethical world. *American Journal of Psychiatry, 146,* 1097–1104.

Freeman, L., & Roy, J. (1976). *Betrayal.* New York: Stein and Day.

Gabbard, G. O. (Ed.). (1989). *Sexual exploitation in professional relationships.* Washington, DC: American Psychiatric Press.

Gabbard, G. O., & Pope, K. S. (1989). Sexual intimacies after termination: Clinical, ethical, and legal aspects. In G. O. Gabbard (Ed.), *Sexual exploitation in professional relationships* (pp. 115–127). Washington, DC: American Psychiatric Press.

Gandhi, M. K. (1948). *Non-violence in peace and war.* Ahmedabadi, India: Narajivan Publishing House.

Gartrell, N., Herman, J., Olarte, S., Feldstein, M., & Localio, R. (1986). Psychiatrist-patient sexual contact: Results of a national survey, I: Prevalence. *American Journal of Psychiatry, 143,* 1126–1131.

Geller, J. D. (1988). Racial bias in the evaluation of patients for psychotherapy. In L. Comas-Dias and E. H. Griffith (Eds.), *Clinical guidelines in cross-cultural mental health* (pp. 112–134). New York: Wiley.

Gibbs, J. C., & Schnell, S. V. (1985). Moral development "versus" socialization: A critique. *American Psychologist, 40,* 1071–1080.

Gibbs, J. T., & Huang, L. N. (1989). *Children of color: Psychological interventions with minority youth.* San Francisco: Jossey-Bass.

Gilligan, C. (1982). *In a different voice: Psychological theory and women's development.* Cambridge, MA: Harvard University Press.

Gilligan, C., Ward, J. V., & Taylor, J. M. (Eds.) with Bardige, B. (1988). *Mapping the moral domain.* Cambridge, MA: Harvard University Press.

Glaser, R. D., & Thorpe, J. S. (1986). Unethical intimacy: A survey of sexual contact and advances between psychology educators and female graduate students. *American Psychologist, 41,* 43–51.

Golding, J. M. (1988). Gender differences in depressive symptoms: Statistical considerations. *Psychology of Women Quarterly, 12,* 61–74.

Goldstein, L. S., & Buongiorno, P. A. (1984). *American Journal of Psychotherapy, 38,* 392–398.

Goleman, D. (1985). *Vital lies, simple truths: The psychology of self-deception.* New York: Simon & Schuster.

Goodyear, R. K., & Sinnett, E. R. (1984). Current and emerging ethical issues for counseling psychology. *Counseling Psychologist, 12,* 87–98.

Gossett, T. F. (1963). *Race: The history of an idea in America.* Dallas: Southern Methodist University Press.

Gould, S. J. (1981). *The mismeasure of man.* New York: Norton.

Grundner, T. M. (1980). On the readability of surgical consent forms. *New England Journal of Medicine, 302,* 900–902.

Guy, J. D., Stark, M. J., & Spolestra, P. A. (1988). Personal therapy for psychologists before and after entering professional practice. *Professional Psychology: Reasearch and Practice, 19,* 474–476.

Guze, S. B., & Robins, E. (1970). Suicide and primary affective disorders. *British Journal of Psychiatry, 117,* 437–438.

Hall, C. S. (1952). Crooks, codes, and cant. *American Psychologist, 1952, 7,* 430–431.

Hall, J. E., & Hare-Mustin, R. T. (1983). Sanctions and the diversity of complaints against psychologists. *American Psychologist, 38,* 714–729.

Hallinan v. Committee of Bar Examiners of State Bar, 55 Cal. Rptr. 228 (1966).

Hamilton, V. L., Blumenfeld, P. C., & Kushler, R. H. (1988). A question of standards: Attributions of blame and credit for classroom acts. *Journal of Personality and Social Psychology, 54,* 34–48.

Handler, J. F. (1990). *Law and the search for community.* Philadelphia: University of Pennsylvania Press.

Harding, S. S., Shearn, M. L., & Kitchener, K. S. (1989, August). *Dual role dilemmas: Psychology educators and their students.* Paper presented at the annual meeting of the American Psychological Association, New Orleans.

Helman, I. D., Morrison, T. L., & Abramowitz, S. I. (1987). Therapist flexibility/rigidity and work stress. *Professional Psychology: Research and Practice, 18,* 21–27.

Herman, J. L., Gartrell, N., Olarte, S., Feldstein, M., & Localio, R. (1987). Psychiatrist-patient sexual contact: Results of a national survey, II: Psychiatrists' attitudes. *American Journal of Psychiatry, 144,* 164–169.

Hobbs, N. (1948). The development of a code of ethical standards for psychology. *American Psychologist, 3,* 80–84.

Hogan, D. B. (1979). *The regulation of psychotherapists.* Cambridge, MA: Ballinger.

Holroyd, J. C., & Brodsky, A. M. (1977). Psychologists' attitudes and practices regarding erotic and nonerotic physical contact with clients. *American Psychologist, 32,* 843–849.

Holroyd, J. C., & Brodsky, A. M. (1980). Does touching patients lead to sexual intercourse? *Professional Psychology, 11,* 807–811.

Indiana General Assembly, House Enrolled Act #1830, Section F (1984).

Irwin, M., Lovitz, A., Marder, S. R., Mintz, J., Winslade, W. J., Van Putten, T., & Mills, M. J. (1985). Psychotic patients' understanding of informed consent. *American Journal of Psychiatry, 142,* 1351–1354.

Isherwood, J., Adam, K. S., & Hornblow, A. R. (1982). Life event stress, psychosocial factors, suicide attempt and auto-accident proclivity. *Journal of Psychosomatic Research, 26,* 371–383.

Jablonski v. United States, 712 F.2d 391 (1983).

James v. Turner, 184 Tenn. 563, 201 S.W. 2d 691 (1942).

Janis, I. L. (1982) *Stress, attitudes, and decisions.* New York: Praeger.

Jones, E. E., & Korchin, S. J. (1982). Minority mental health: Perspectives. In E. E. Jones and S. J. Korchin (Eds.), *Minority mental health* (pp. 3–36). New York: Praeger.

Jones, J. H. (1981). *Bad blood: The Tuskegee syphilis experiment — A tragedy of race and medicine.* New York: Free Press.

Jones, J. M. (1990a, September 14). Promoting diversity in an individualistic society. Keynote address, Great Lakes College Association conference, "Multiculturalism transforming the 21st century: Overcoming the challenges and preparing for the future." Hope College, Holland, MI.

Jones, J. M. (1990b, August). *Psychological approaches to race: What have they been and what should they be?* Paper presented at the annual meeting of the American Psychological Association, Boston.

Jones, J. M., & Block, C. B. (1984). Black cultural perspectives. *The Clinical Psychologist, 37,* 58–62.

Kahneman, D., Slovic, P., & Tversky, A. (1982). *Judgment under uncertainty: Heuristics and biases.* Cambridge: Cambridge University Press.

Kazdin, A. E. (1983). Hopelessness, depression, and suicidal intent among psychiatrically disturbed inpatient children. *Journal of Consulting and Clinical Psychology, 51,* 504–510.

Keith-Spiegel, P., & Koocher, G. P. (1985). *Ethics in psychology.* New York: Random House.

Kelman, H. C., & Hamilton, V. L. (1989). *Crimes of obedience: Toward a social psychology of authority and responsibility.* New Haven, CT: Yale University Press.

Kent v. Whitaker, 58 Wash. 2d 569, 364 P.2d 556 (1961).

Kilburg, R. R., Nathan, P. E., & Thoreson, R. W. (Eds.). (1986). *Professionals in distress: Issues, syndromes, and solutions in psychology.* Washington, DC: American Psychological Association.

King, M. L., Jr. (1958). *Stride toward freedom.* San Francisco: Harper & Row.

King, M. L., Jr. (1964). *Why we can't wait.* New York: Signet.

Kleespies, P. M., Smith, M. R., & Becker, B. R. (1990). Psychology interns as patient suicide survivors: Incidence, impact, and recovery. *Professional Psychology: Research and Practice, 21,* 257–263.

Klerman, G. L., & Clayton, P. (1984). Epidemiologic perspectives on the health consequences of bereavement. In M. Osterweis, F. Solomon, & M. Green (Eds.), *Bereavement: Reactions, consequences, and care* (pp. 15–44). Washington, DC: National Academy Press.

Kohlberg, L. (1969). *Stages in development of moral thought and action.* New York: Holt.

Kovacs, A. L. (1987, May). Insurance billing: The growing risk of lawsuits against psychologists. *The Independent Practitioner, 7,* 21–24.

Kramer, M., Pollack, E. S., Redick, R. W., & Locke, B. Z. (1972). *Mental disorders/Suicide.* Cambridge, MA: Harvard University Press.

Krupnick, J. L. (1984). Bereavement during childhood and adolescence. In M. Osterweis, F. Solomon, & M. Green (Eds.), *Bereavement: Reactions, consequences, and care* (pp. 99–141). Washington, DC: National Academy Press.

LaFromboise, T. D., & Foster, S. L. (1989). Ethics and multicultural counseling. In P. D. Pedersen, J. G. Draguns, W. J. Lonner, & E. J. Trimble (Eds.), *Counseling across cultures* (3rd ed.). (pp. 115-136). Honolulu: University of Hawaii Press.

Langer, E. J. (1989). *Mindfulness.* Reading, MA: Addison-Wesley.

Langer, E. J., & Abelson, R. P. (1974). A patient by any other name . . . : Clinician group differences and labeling bias. *Journal of Consulting and Clinical Psychology, 42,* 4–9.

Langer, E. J., Bashner, R., & Chanowitz, B. (1985). Decreasing prejudice by increasing discrimination. *Journal of Personality and Social Psychology, 49,* 113–120.

Lehner, G. F. J. (1952). Defining psychotherapy. *American Psychologist, 7,* 547.

Lettieri, D. J. (1982). Suicidal death prediction scales. In P. A. Keller & L. G. Ritt (Eds.), *Innovations in clinical practice: Vol. 1* (pp. 265–268). Sarasota, FL: Professional Resource Exchange.

Levenson, H., & Pope, K. S. (1981). First encounters: Effects of intake procedures on patients, staff, and the organization. *Hospital and Community Psychiatry, 32,* 482–485.

Levine, R. J. (1988). *Ethics and regulation of clinical research* (2nd ed.). New Haven, CT: Yale University Press.

Lickona, T. (Ed.). (1976). *Moral development and behavior: Theory, research, and social issues.* New York: Holt.

Litman, R. E. (1965). When patients commit suicide. *American Journal of Psychotherapy, 19,* 570–583.

A little recent history. (1952). *American Psychologist, 7,* 425.

Livermore, J., Malmquist, C., & Meehl, P. (1968). On the justification for civil commitment. *University of Pennsylvania Law Review, 117,* 75–96.

Masters, W. H., & Johnson, V. E. (1966). *Human sexual response.* New York: Bantam.

Masters, W. H., & Johnson, V. E. (1970). *Human sexual inadequacy.* New York: Bantam.

Masters, W. H., & Johnson, V. E. (1975, May). *Principles of the new sex therapy.* Paper presented at the annual meeting of the American Psychiatric Association, Anaheim, CA.

Masters, W. H., & Johnson, V. E. (1976). Principles of the new sex therapy. *American Journal of Psychiatry, 110,* 3370–3373.

Masterson, J. F. (1989, May). Maintaining objectivity crucial in treating borderline patients. *Psychiatric Times,* pp. 1, 26–27.

McCartney, J. (1966). Overt transference. *Journal of Sex Research, 2,* 227–237.

McCord, C., & Freeman, H. P. (1990). Excess mortality in Harlem. *New England Journal of Medicine, 322,* 173–177.

McKelvey v. Turnage, U.S. Supreme Court, 86–737 (April 20, 1988).

McNeil, B., Pauker, S. G., Sox, H. C., & Tversky, A. (1982). On the elucidation of preferences for alternative therapies. *New England Journal of Medicine, 306,* 1259–1262.

Mednick, M. T. (1989). On the politics of psychological constructs: Stop the bandwagon, I want to get off. *American Psychologist, 44,* 1118–1123.

Mercer, J. R. (1979). *Technical manual: System of multicultural pluralistic assessment.* New York: Psychological Corporation.

Milgram, S. (1974). *Obedience to authority: An experimental view.* New York: Harper & Row.

Mintz, N. L. (1971). Patient fees and psychotherapeutic transactions. *Journal of Consulting and Clinical Psychology, 43,* 835–841.

Monahan, J. (Ed.). (1980). *Who is the client?* Washington, DC: American Psychological Association.

Morra v. State Board of Examiners of Psychologists, 510 Kans. P.2d 614 (1973).

Murphy, J. M. (1976). Psychiatric labeling in cross-cultural perspective. *Science, 191,* 1019–1028.

Natanson v. Kline, 186 Kans. 393, 406, 350 P.2d 1093 (1960).

National Association of Social Workers. (1989). *Standards for the practice of clinical social work.* Silver Springs, MD: Author.

National Association of Social Workers. (1990). *Code of ethics* (rev. ed.). Silver Springs, MD: Author.

Neisser, U. (1981). John Dean's memory. *Cognition, 9,* 1–22.

Neuringer, C. (1964). Rigid thinking in suicidal individuals. *Journal of Consulting Psychology, 28,* 54–58.

Neuringer, C. (1974). *Psychological assessment of suicidal risk.* New York: Charles Thomas.

Patsiokas, A. T., Clum, G. A., & Luscumb, R. L. (1979). Cognitive characteristics of suicidal attempters. *Journal of Consulting and Clinical Psychology, 47,* 478–484.

Peck, M., & Seiden, R. (1975, May). Youth suicide. *exChange* (California State Department of Health), pp. 17–20.

Pedersen, P. D., Draguns, J. G., Lonner, W. J., & Trimble, E. J. (1989). Introduction and overview. In P. D. Pedersen, J. G. Draguns, W. J. Lonner, & E. J. Trimble (Eds.), *Counseling across cultures* (3rd ed.) (pp. 1–2). Honolulu: University of Hawaii Press.

Pederson, D., Shinedling, M., & Johnson, D. (1975). Effects of sex of examiner and subject on children's quantitative test performance. In R. K. Unger and F. Denmark (Eds.), *Women: Dependent or independent variable?* (pp. 410–472). New York: Psychological Dimensions.

People v. Gomez, App., 185 Cal. Rptr. 155 (August 10, 1982).

People v. Stritzinger, 194 Cal. Rptr. 431 (Cal. September 1, 1983).

People v. Younghanz, 202 Cal. Rptr. 907 (Cal. App. 4 Dist. May 31, 1984).

Perspectives. (1990, April 23). *Newsweek,* p. 17.

Petrie, K., & Chamberlain, K. (1983). Hopelessness and social desirability as moderator variables in predicting suicidal behavior. *Journal of Consulting and Clinical Psychology, 51,* 485–487.

Plaisil, E. (1985). *Therapist.* New York: St. Martin's/Marek.

Plato. (1956a). The apology. In E. H. Harrington & P. G. Rouse (Eds.), *Great dialogues of Plato* (W. H. D. Rouse, Trans., pp. 423–446). New York: New American Library.

Plato. (1956b). Crito. In E. H. Harrington & P. G. Rouse (Eds.), *Great dialogues of Plato* (W. H. D. Rouse, Trans., pp. 447–459). New York: New American Library.

Pope, K. S. (1986, November). New trends in malpractice cases and changes in APA liability insurance. *The Independent Practitioner, 6,* 23–26.

Pope, K. S. (1988a). Dual relationships: A source of ethical, legal, and clinical problems. *Independent Practitioner, 8* (1), 17–25.

Pope, K. S. (1988b). How clients are harmed by sexual contact with mental health professionals: The syndrome and its prevalence. *Journal of Counseling and Development, 67,* 222–226.

Pope, K. S. (1989a). Malpractice suits, licensing disciplinary actions, and ethics cases: Frequencies, causes, and costs. *Independent Practitioner, 9*(1), 22–26.

Pope, K. S. (1989b). Student-teacher sexual intimacy. In G. O. Gabbard (Ed.), *Sexual exploitation within professional relationships* (pp. 163–176). Washington, DC: American Psychiatric Press.

Pope, K. S. (1990a). Ethical and malpractice issues in hospital practice. *American Psychologist, 45,* 1066–1070.

Pope, K. S. (1990b). Therapist-patient sex as sex abuse: six scientific, professional, and practical dilemmas in addressing victimization and rehabilitation. *Professional Psychology: Research and Practice, 21,* 227–239.

Pope, K. S. (1990c). Therapist-patient sexual involvement: A review of the research. *Clinical Psychology Review, 10,* 477–490.

Pope, K. S., & Bajt, T. R. (1988). When laws and values conflict: A dilemma for psychologists. *American Psychologist, 43,* 828.

Pope, K. S., & Bouhoutsos, J. C. (1986). *Sexual intimacy between therapists and patients.* New York: Praeger.

Pope, K. S., & Gabbard, G. O. (1989). Individual psychotherapy for victims of therapist-patient sexual intimacy. In G. O. Gabbard (Ed.), *Sexual exploitation in professional relationships* (pp. 89–100). Washington, DC: American Psychiatric Press.

Pope, K. S., Keith-Spiegel, P., & Tabachnick, B. G. (1986). Sexual attraction to clients: The human therapist and the (sometimes) inhuman training system. *American Psychologist, 41,* 147–158.

Pope, K. S., Levenson, H., & Schover, L. R. (1979). Sexual intimacy in psychology training: Results and implications of a national survey. *American Psychologist, 34,* 682–689.

Pope, K. S., & Morin, S. F. (1990). AIDS and HIV infection update: New research, ethical responsibilities, evolving legal frameworks, and published resources. *Independent Practitioner, 10,* pp. 43–53.

Pope, K. S., Simpson, N. H., & Weiner, M. F. (1978). Malpractice in psychotherapy. *American Journal of Psychotherapy, 32,* 593–602.

Pope, K. S., Tabachnick, B. G., & Keith-Spiegel, P. (1987). Ethics of practice: The beliefs and behaviors of psychologists as therapists. *American Psychologist, 42,* 993–1006.

Pope, K. S., Tabachnick, B. G., & Keith-Spiegel, P. (1988). Good and poor practices in psychotherapy: National survey of beliefs of psychologists. *Professional Psychology: Research and Practice, 19,* 547–552.

Pope, K. S., & Vetter, V. A. (in press). Prior therapist-patient sexual involvement among patients seen by psychologists. *Psychotherapy.*

Rachlin, H. (1989). *Judgment, decision, and choice: A cognitive/behavioral synthesis:* New York: W.H. Freeman.

Reiser, D. E., & Levenson, H. (1984). Abuses of the borderline diagnosis: a clinical problem with teaching opportunities. *American Journal of Psychiatry, 141,* 1528–1532.

Ridley, C. R. (1989). Racism in counseling as adversive behavioral process. In P. B. Pedersen, J. G. Draguns, W. J. Lonner, & J. E. Trimble (Eds.), *Counseling across cultures* (3rd ed.; pp. 55–78). Honolulu: University of Hawaii Press.

Rivers, E., Schuman, S., Simpson, L., & Olansky, S. (1953). Twenty years of followup experience in a long-range medical study. *Public Health Reports, 68,* 391–395.

Robinson, G., & Merav, A. (1976). Informed consent: Recall by patients tested postoperatively. *Annals of Thoracic Surgery, 22,* 209–212.

Robinson, W. L., & Reid, P. T. (1985). Sexual intimacies in psychology revisited. *Professional Psychology, 16,* 512–520.

Sahagun, L. (1988, November 6). Diary of rape victim in therapy is focus of legal dispute. *Los Angeles Times,* p. 43.

Sanders, J. R., & Keith-Spiegel, P. (1980). Formal and informal adjudication of ethics complaints against psychologists. *American Psychologist, 35,* 1096–1105.

Sarason, S. B. (1985). *Caring and compassion in clinical practice.* San Francisco: Jossey-Bass.

Scarr, S., & Weinberg, R. A. (1976). IQ test performance of black children adopted by white families. *American Psychologist, 30,* 726–739.

Schloendorf v. Society of New York Hospital, 211 N.Y. 125, 105 N.E. 92 (1914).

Schneidman, E. (1975). Suicide. In A. M. Freedman, H. I. Kaplan, & B. J. Saddock (Eds.), *Comprehensive textbook of psychiatry* (pp. 1774–1784). Baltimore, MD: Williams & Wilkins.

Schneidman, E. (1976). *Suicidology: Contemporary developments.* New York: Grune & Stratton.

Schulyer, D. (1974). *The depressive spectrum.* New York: Jason Aronson.

Shapiro, D. L. (1990). *Forensic psychological assessment: An integrative approach.* Boston: Allyn & Bacon.

Shaver, K. G., & Drown, D. (1986). On causality, responsibility, and self-blame: A theoretical note. *Journal of Personality and Social Psychology, 50,* 697–702.

Singer, J. L. (1980). The scientific basis of psychotherapeutic practice: A question of values and ethics. *Psychotherapy: Theory, research and practice, 17,* 372–383.

Smith, S. H., & Whitehead, G. I. (1988). The public and private use of consensus-raising excuses. *Journal of Personality, 56,* 355–371.

Sonne, J. L. (1987). Proscribed sex: Counseling the patient subjected to sexual intimacy by a therapist. *Medical Aspects of Human Sexuality, 16,* 18–23.

Sonne, J. L. (1989). An example of group therapy for victims of therapist-client sexual intimacy. In G. O. Gabbard (Ed.), *Sexual exploitation in professional relationships* (pp. 101–127). Washington, DC: American Psychiatric Press.

Sonne, J. L., Meyer, C. B., Borys, D., & Marshall, V. (1985). Clients' reaction to sexual intimacy in therapy. *American Journal of Orthopsychiatry, 55,* 183–189.

Sonne, J. L., & Pope, K. S. (in press). Treating victims of therapist-patient sexual involvement. [Special issue]. *Psychotherapy.*

Standards for educational and psychological testing. (1985). Washington, DC: American Psychological Association.

Stanton, W. (1960). *The leopard's spots: Scientific attitudes toward race in America.* Chicago: University of Chicago Press.

Stevens, N. (1990, August 25). Did I say average? I meant superior. *New York Times,* p. 15.

Stoltenberg, C. D., & Delworth, U. (1987). *Supervising counselors and therapists.* San Francisco: Jossey-Bass.

Stone, A. A. (1978, March 19). Mentally ill: To commit or not, that is the question. *New York Times,* p. 10-E.

Stone, M. T. (1982). Turning points in psychotherapy. In S. Slipp (Ed.), *Curative factors in dynamic psychotherapy* (pp. 259–279). New York: McGraw-Hill.

Stromberg, C. D., Haggarty, R. F., McMillian, M. H., Mishkin, B., Rubin, B. L., & Trilling, H. R. (1988). *The psychologist's legal handbook.* Washington, DC: Council for the National Register of Health Service Providers in Psychology.

Tallman, G. (1981). *Therapist-client social relationships.* Unpublished manuscript, California State University, Northridge.

Tavris, C. (1987, November 1). Method is all but lost in the imagery of social-science fiction. *Los Angeles Times,* Section V, p. 5.

Thomas, A., & Sillen, S. (1972). *Racism and psychiatry.* Secaucus, NJ: Citadel Press.

Thoreau, H. D. (1960). *Walden and civil disobedience.* Boston: Houghton Mifflin. (*Civil disobedience* originally published 1849)

Thoreson, R. W., Miller, M., & Krauskopf, C. J. (1989). The distressed psychologist: Prevalence and treatment considerations. *Professional Psychology: Research and Practice, 20,* 153–158.

Tolstoy, L. (1951). *The kingdom of God is within you* (L. Weiner, Trans.). Boston: Page. (Originally published 1894)

Traynor v. Turnage, U.S. Supreme Court, 86-622, April 20, 1988.

Truman v. Thomas, California, 611 P.2d 902, 27 Cal. 3d 285. (1980).

Tsuang, M. T. (1983). Risk of suicide in relatives of schizophrenics, manics, depressives, and controls. *Journal of Clinical Psychiatry, 39,* 396–400.

U.S. Public Health Service. (1973). *Final report of the Tuskegee syphilis study ad hoc advisory panel.* Washington, DC: Author.

Vinson, J. S. (1987). Use of complaint procedures in cases of therapist-patient sexual contact. *Professional Psychology: Research and Practice, 18,* 159–164.

Walker v. City of Birmingham, 388 U.S. 307, 18 L ed 2d 1210 (1967).

Walker, E., & Young, T. D. (1986). *A killing cure.* New York: Holt.

Weiner, I. B. (1988, August). *Can a psychological assessment do what we think it can?* Paper presented at the annual meeting of the American Psychological Association, Atlanta.

Weiner, I. B. (1989). On competence and ethicality in psychodiagnostic assessment. *Journal of Personality Assessment, 53,* 827–831.

Weisman, A. D., & Worden, J. W. (1972). Risk-rescue rating in suicide assessment. *Archives of General Psychiatry, 26,* 553–560.

Westermeyer, J. (1987). Cultural factors in clinical assessment. *Journal of Consulting and Clinical Psychology, 55,* 471–478.

Wetzel, R. (1976). Hopelessness, depression, and suicide intent. *Archives of General Psychiatry, 33,* 1069–1073.

Word, C., Zanna, M. P., & Cooper, J. (1974). The nonverbal mediation of self-fulfilling prophecies in interracial interaction. *Journal of Experimental Social Psychology, 10,* 109–120.

Ziskin, J. (1981). *Coping with psychiatric and psychological expert testimony.* Venice, CA: Law and Psychology Press.

Index